True Stories of the Supernatural

Greg Holland

TRILOGY CHRISTIAN PUBLISHERS

TUSTIN, CA

Trilogy Christian Publishers

A Wholly Owned Subsidary of Trinity Broadcasting Network

2442 Michelle Drive

Tustin, CA 92780

Cover design by: Jeff Summers

For information about special discounts for bulk purchases, please contact Trilogy Christian Publishing.

Manufactured in the United States of America

10 9 8 7 6 5 4 3 2 1

Library of Congress Cataloging-in-Publication Data is available.

ISBN: 978-1-63769-954-6

E-ISBN: 978-1-63769-955-3

Endorsements

What an ordeal you guys have been through, yet even in the midst of the struggle, I sit amazed at your writing. Your written word is artwork, simply lovely.

—Oakette, homemaker

It was so wonderful and wondrous to read the stories. The one with the eagles inspired and encouraged me that we were soaring higher and wiser. As you shared the stories, I can hear the calm assurance of the Father's voice. The wisdom, lessons, and inspiration speak and confirm things to me from His heart.

—Jeanie Richardson, co-pastor
Firepoint Church, Tujunga, California

I have had the privilege of experiencing and living out these stories with my parents. Throughout my life, I have learned that no matter what, God is in control, and more often than not, the answers are simple, and the miracles—big or small—will always come.

These stories are entertaining, but I also hope they inspire you, motivate you, and that you will be able to take away something that will help you in this adventure of life.

—Travis Holland, US Navy EOD, son of the author

Growing up in an environment of spiritual warfare and watching my father and mother stand in such belief/faith that no matter what comes against us, no matter what lies before us, no matter what—God will always do the miraculous!

I have watched my family grow through the stories you are about to read, and I know that if you pray, believe, and stand on the Word of God, He will do the same for you.

—Garrett Holland fitness professional, son of the author

After reading this book, you will understand why I personally have such faith in God. Growing up, I've known that everything is ultimately in God's hands, but the power of prayer is so real. Every time I've needed prayer throughout my life, my father would pray for me, and I would immediately have peace of mind about it. In each situation, no matter what, the outcome was always in my favor. These stories will capture you; they are truly powerful and inspiring.

—Bryce Holland, US Marine Corps, son of the author

Contents

Foreword

These are enlightening stories of intensity, strength, passion, pain, love, heartbreak, miracles, and victory.

Fear of the unknown is dispelled when you are led by the voice of the Holy Spirit. These stories are simple yet extraordinarily powerful. If we step back and open our eyes to the reality of how the natural and supernatural work together in our daily lives, we'd be far more successful and have a lot more fun in this life's journey.

Greg Holland has opened a window to his life experiences and that of his family, friends, and others he has ministered to. We can enjoy a look into the help, healing, and strength that is available to us all for overcoming, success, and victory in our daily walk through life.

Get ready for adventure, fun, and breakthrough in these true-life stories.

—Michelle Holland

Introduction

Why write this book? I wanted to inspire others to walk in their giftings and callings. I wanted to inspire others to make an effort to walk closer to God. I want people to know that no matter who they are and what they do or don't know that anyone can learn to hear God better, anyone can learn how to pray, and anyone can actually see results from those prayers. Anyone!

Life is a journey, and prayer just makes things better. I want to inspire people to know that when they pray that God hears them, cares about their circumstances no matter how small, no matter how impossible, and that He can and will help them.

I have seen it so many times in my life that there is no doubt in my mind anymore that God loves me and that He will perform His Word in my situation, and things will turn out better than if I hadn't prayed. I want to inspire others to try it for themselves. I want people to see that it's not a religion, it's a lifestyle, it's not just a lifestyle, it's a relationship.

It is a relationship that is formed by spending time reading the Bible, then praying about the issues of your life, then spending time listening to what the Holy Spirit says to you. What guidance does He have for you, what revelation is He wanting to share with you? Learning that you don't have to have someone else hear for you but that you can hear for yourself.

It's like that old saying, "How do you eat an elephant? One bite at a time!" How do you learn all this stuff? One day at a time, one verse at a time, one experience at a time, and next thing you know, you're having successes in your life; you're beginning to have victories where you didn't before.

I want people to read these stories and be inspired to take action in their own lives. I want them to see that if it worked for me, then it will work for them. Like it says that God is no respecter of persons, which basically means that He's just as willing to help you as He is to help me or any other person on the planet, regardless of who you think you aren't.

He loves you, and He will help you too. I want people to know that the Bible is about your everyday life. The dirty dishes, the car problems, the pain, the issues at work, your mother-in-law. The struggles and problems we all face, some small, some life-threatening, the Lord cares about them all. He has answers and deliverance from every situation you come up against. No part of your life is too small for the Lord, and no part is too big for Him.

I realize that some of these stories seem too fantastic or impossible, even unbelievable. And you would be right; they do seem that way. I wouldn't blame you for questioning what's true and what isn't. But they all happened. They happened to one or more person in my immediate family, and they happened over the course of many years.

I want to encourage you that everyone has their own stories, and every story is a part of your testimony. Something that is unique to you, and because of that, it will speak specifically to the people around you, the people in your life.

It says numerous times in Revelation, in the messages to the churches, that to him who overcomes, there are rewards, and good things will happen to you. Our stories, yours and mine, are about victories both large and small, but even more than that, they are about overcoming, overcoming the obstacles and problems and evil in life, overcoming because of the blood of the Lamb and because of the word of our testimony like it says in Revelation 12:11, being a victor and not a victim.

Our testimonies are about something bigger than we are, something that wouldn't have happened without supernatural intervention in our lives on some level. God wants to use our testimonies to help others to be successful and to overcome. So may my stories do that for you. And may you be that success, may you be that overcomer whose life speaks to others to encourage and inspire, in Jesus' name.

The Fox

I was getting wood for the fire. The porch light illuminated the front yard and the path to the woodshed like a tunnel through the dark. The contrast between the black night and the white of the sparkling new snow was stunning. Stopping to enjoy the sight, I breathed in the fresh, crisp, Rocky Mountain air and marveled at the peace that comes with perfect silence.

Earlier that week, I had read about the incredible friendly encounters the first Irish Christians had with animals. Like the otters who snuggled up and kept a man warm while he laid on the bank after he stood praying in the middle of a cold river. Or the boy who requested milk and a doe came each day to provide it. Or the eagle that brought a man a large fish every few days, so he had something to eat.

I thought how wonderful those encounters were and had even prayed silently that the Lord might do such a thing for me—not really knowing what it might entail.

Stepping slowly up the old stone steps, I had a feeling to turn around. Some movement got my attention in the dark beyond the reach of the light. Small quick footsteps disturbed the peace. Peering intently through the softly falling snow, I tried to determine what was out there. What could possibly be stirring on a night like tonight? Soon a figure came trotting into the light. At first, I thought it was a large cat. A cat? Hmmm, how strange. But as it came closer towards me, I realized it was a small fox.

He came up the steps right to my boots, looking up into my face like he was trying to tell me something. Stopping, he settled back onto his haunches and kept looking up at me. His fur coat looked warm and comfortable, with glistening snowflakes caught on the end of almost every hair. Looking into his eyes, it was like I could see the wildness within him flickering behind the curiosity on his face, and then there was this unusual peace that just emanated from him.

My next impulse was to reach down and touch him. But something inside me said very strongly, "No, don't do it." Just then, he rose up slowly on his hind legs leading with his nose until it touched the forearm of my coat. Time seemed suspended as I stood motionless, and he sniffed back and forth from my elbow to my wrist. Seemingly satisfied, he sat back down on his haunches and continued looking up at me like he still wanted to tell me something. The look on his face was like I should understand. I wondered intently what he was trying to say.

Not wanting to keep this experience to myself any longer, I called out to my wife. "Michelle, quick, come look at this." Hoping she could hear me from inside the house. Hoping it wouldn't scare the fox off.

But it did. Darting away, he stopped at the edge of the light and looked back as if still trying to communicate something. Then he turned and disappeared into the night as quickly and softly as he had come, leaving only his tracks as a testimony of what had just happened. Wow! What an experience. What an amazing experience.

Then inside me, I heard a voice, "Remember what you prayed concerning the ancient Irish and their relationship with animals." *How wonderful,* I thought. *The Lord had answered my simple prayer.*

Michelle and the Bear

Michelle said goodbye to me as I left for work; she went into the house to get her freshly made burrito and return outside to eat it. With burrito in hand, she stepped out on the front porch walking down a few steps to savor it, enjoying the warm, sunny fall day. The trees were starting to turn colors; the birds were happily singing all around her, and life was teeming everywhere. She stretched out so as to take in all the life and goodness around when she noticed something odd over by the woodshed. A bear. What! A bear? Right here in our front yard?

We had just been studying Genesis 1:28 where it talks about our dominion over every living thing. One of the promises that Jesus restored to us. You know where it says:

"And God blessed them; and God said to them 'Be fruitful and multiply, and fill the earth, and subdue it; and rule over the fish of the sea and over the birds of the sky, and over every living thing that moves on the earth.'"

Without missing a beat, she pointed her half-eaten burrito at him and yelled, "You don't belong here, go on, leave now in Jesus' name." A look of uncertainty and fear came across his face, and he slowly turned and started to walk up the mountain, then stopped and looked back, questioning. He then lifted his head, turned, and sniffed the air like he just smelled something really appealing. Appealing enough to stop a bear in his tracks. Still sniffing the air, he stared intently towards Michelle. No longer unsure.

She realized he was smelling her burrito. Now she had become the target. Running up the stairs back into the house, she laid lunch on the counter then burst back out the front door.

All right, Mr. Bear, where'd you go? She walked around, scanning the hillside for any sign of him. Hmmm, no bear. Then she saw them. Ears. Two bear ears sticking up just above the chokecherry thicket about thirty yards away. Looking more closely, she could see his beady little eyes peering through the tangled brush at her. He thought he was hidden; he didn't realize his ears were showing. At least that's what we thought that he thought.

Anyway, she commanded that he leave in the name of Jesus again, and this time, he ran all the way up the mountain and disappeared. *Wow!* she thought. *I felt the power and dominion of the Word, and I expected this bear to obey, and he did.* The name of Jesus works on animals just as God said. Boy, did this experience expand our belief system.

You Still Have a Voice (An Experience with Death)

"Michelle, look at this, quick, come here, hurry, or you'll miss it. All right, in the back, there under the sheets, doesn't that look like a body, doesn't that look like an arm sticking up?" This guy came through our drive-thru every morning right after we opened, sometimes in an old station wagon, sometimes in a van, and he always had really suspicious things covered up under the sheets in the back. I mean, it always looked like he had one or more bodies lying in the back. He doesn't look like a drug dealer, and he doesn't look like he's in the mafia, so what is he, and why does he always have what looks like bodies in the back of his car? That's a little creepy, don't you think?

We saw him enough to realize we were right, and those really were bodies in the back. One time there was this hand sticking out from under the sheet with the fingers pointed towards the sky. If that didn't verify our suspicions, I don't know what would have.

I couldn't take it anymore; after many days of seeing dead bodies covered with sheets nonchalantly going through the drive-thru, I had to ask. Mustering all the tact I could, one morning, I finally blurted out, "So what's with all the bodies in the back of your car?"

"Oh, I'm a mortician, and I offer pick-up services at peoples' homes. So all the bodies you've seen are people who recently died at home, and I just went and picked them up for the families so I could prepare them for burial," he chuckled, and with a twinkle in his eye, he drove off.

Standing there speechless, I couldn't respond because his answer took me totally off guard. I mean, we were sure he was some kind of hitman or something and was getting rid of the evidence. A mortician? Wow, the most simple, practical answer, and we didn't even come close with all our supposing and conjecturing; actually, hitman sounded a lot more interesting and mysterious. Who would have thought, a mortician? Can you imagine what his car must have smelled like?

Over the weeks, we developed a pleasant relationship with him, and he would tell us mortician jokes; gosh, everybody has their own jokes, even morticians. We got to where we would look forward to his arrival every morning. Like many of our regulars, he was a joy to interact with.

One day out of the blue, he told Michelle, "You know, you should come by the mortuary someday, and I'll show you what we do." So she did.

When she pulled up to a parking space in front of the building, her mind was full of questions. She wondered, "What am I going to see, and do I even want to see it?" Curiosity took over, and she got out and carefully went through the front door, not sure what she would find. Morti (that's what we called him, is short for mortician) met her inside and was so excited that someone was actually interested in his work. Taking Michelle through the whole place, he showed her everything, happily explaining what was going on at each stage of preparation of the bodies for burial.

You know we don't realize it, but somebody has to do this job, and most of us would never even consider it. Everyone that's born is going to die, and someone has to take care of all the bodies. But Morti came right out and proudly proclaimed that this is what he is called to do. Both his father and grandfather were morticians, and he knew from the time he was little that this was what he wanted to do. God has a place for everyone, doesn't He? He spoke about how he loves doing this job and that he is really good at it. To him, it was like art. When he was finished, he could look at his work and be proud of what he had just done. The real proof, of course, was when the family would come in and marvel at how well the person looked and how thankful they were and what a wonderful job the mortician had done. It always gave him great joy to see how he was able to do his part in helping people through this difficult transition of life. And to be able to do it well. Really well.

Entering a large room, Morti began explaining about the four bodies that were in different stages of preparation for their funerals. One had Vaseline caked all over her face.

"What's this?" Michelle inquired.

"Oh, it's a woman who was some kind of preacher, and her family wanted to wait a couple of weeks to have time to gather all the people for the funeral. I guess she had quite a following. The Vaseline all over her face is to preserve it, so it looks as natural as possible when the people finally see her."

"But won't she start looking bad?" Michelle asked.

"That's what the Vaseline is for, and there are some other things I can do when the time comes. It helps preserve the skin. And yes, there is a limit to how long we can hold them before we finally have to bury them." Thankfully there was no bad smell.

As Michelle looked at the four dead bodies, she heard the Holy Spirit down inside, "They have no more voice." *Interesting,* she noted to herself, *I'll have to think about that.*

"I was amazed that I didn't feel sad or bad, just interested in who they might have been, how they loved and who loved them, how they lived and how they died," Michelle said later. She felt a caution not to get too close like she could look but not touch. Why? Who knows? Of course, she didn't really want to touch them anyway; she already knew what a dead person felt like. Cold and hard, no life left at all. She didn't know any of the people, so she could gaze at them and feel nothing, no emotion at all, just wonder and curiosity. Maybe that's how the mortician felt; maybe that's how he deals with death and the dead day in and day out without going crazy.

Morti turned and intently studied her face looking to see how this was all affecting her. Satisfied that all was well, he took her to the next place of interest, the crematory. In a way, it was like being in a haunted house that wasn't haunted. There was nothing evil about it, just an odd, weird kind of feeling like that.

On the next table was a little tiny grandmother in a cardboard box; the box was a part of the casket. He said that this is what they put them in if they are to be cremated, though when the people view them, they are in a real casket. She had pictures and poems and fondly remembered things laid carefully around her from loved ones. He said that all these things would be cremated with her; they will go with her to the grave. Michelle pondered how incredibly final death is; she could tell that this woman was greatly loved. She suddenly felt sad for her family, sorry for their loss. She could tell this woman had given much into her family, they would miss her presence, but her influence and the valuable and precious things she gave into their lives would stay with them forever.

Then he showed Michelle the tiny grandmother was next to go into the oven. There was a huge silver door in the wall; behind it was the vault where the bodies are cremated, one at a time. She could hear the flames burning and what sounded like water splashing into the fire behind it. Curious, she asked, "What is that sound?"

Morti turned to her and said, "Well, we have a large person being cremated, and that sound is the bodily fluids and fat being burned."

She thought that was quite weird as the reality struck her that she was listening to a dead body being burned, it was an everyday part of Morti's job, but it was something we would never ponder. She was glad to know that their spirit was gone, that there was no feeling, no pain.

He then said, "Come on, I'll show you the freezer." As he opened the door, a whoosh of cold air blew across their faces.

Inside she saw there were three walls lined with four shelves each from the floor to the ceiling, a blue-tinted room of stainless steel shelves with ice white bodies wrapped in white sheets. Each person had a tag on their toes, and if they didn't have toes, it was on their ankle, and it had a date and the time listed for each cremation which then matched the schedule on the wall— quite the business.

He said, "There is one more place I should show you that may be part of a cremation, and that is the area with the grinder. This is where we have to put the pieces of bone that didn't get burned up and grind them down; sometimes that happens."

It sounded gruesome; Michelle felt he wanted her to react to this. But she didn't react; she just kept a straight face and said, "I never knew there were bones that wouldn't completely burn up."

Seemingly satisfied, he grinned, and turned, and headed back towards the front, so she followed him. He said, "That's the end of the tour," and that we could make an appointment for funeral arrangements sometime.

Michelle just smiled and thanked him and said, "We'll see."

Morti had cancer, so part of his throat had been removed, and he had to talk through a voice machine. He pushed at the bottom of his neck on something like a button when he wanted to speak. It sounded low and gravely, and he said "Sweet dreams" and smiled mischievously. She thought how weird it was for him to say that and how it seemed that he really wanted to scare her. So she just laughed at him and walked out the door and to her car.

"As I stepped back out into the world of sunshine and life, I said in my mind, 'Lord, what was this all about?' I didn't feel scared, but I knew it was a part of the world I couldn't wrap my head around yet; I needed to process what I just experienced," she told me later.

She continued, "I most distinctly heard, 'You have a voice, they don't.' They have no more voice on this earth, but you do. Tell others about Me and use your voice and bring life to others. Tell others the truth. Use your voice. Use your life. Don't waste it. Bring life, enjoy life." She also heard the Holy Spirit say, "You need to tell the people to use their voice for Me on this earth. Your voice is what makes change in your world and speaks into others' lives. When you're dead and gone, you're done. You have no more voice, no more influence. Lift your voice up now while you can because someday you won't be able to anymore. Don't leave any good thing unsaid, any compliment unknown, any love unshared."

"Lift up your voice; speak out now.
Shout it from the rooftops now
for you don't know what tomorrow may bring."

She continued to ponder out loud, "I thought about how sudden and final death is. No one laying there knew when their final breath would be. Yet there they were. Would they have done anything differently had they known? What things did these people not say that they should have? What unspoken love or encouragement will never be known by those they left behind? Mysteries that will never be solved, pain that will never be addressed so it can be healed, hope that was so needed but never shared? This was the biggest pivot point of life that I had ever experienced without any pain or despair attached to it. My thoughts became a movie inside my head. I was already thinking much differently about how I would continue my journey in life. I was happy, I could say, I am alive. I still have a voice."

Psalm 115:17-18
"The dead do not praise the Lord,
Nor *do* any who go down into silence;

But as for us, we will bless the Lord
From this time forth and forever.
Praise the Lord!"

This is a drawing I did of Lot's wife from Genesis 19

Don't Look Back

Looking back
and contemplating things
that should be left behind,
and losing
not only her future
but her life,
losing her family
as her hopes and dreams
turn to salt
and crumble away.
There are things from our past
that are the foundation for our future.
There are things from our past
that should be left behind.
Sometimes it's best if we
leave them there
and we
Don't Look Back.

Spirit in the Living Room

Bryce woke abruptly from his sleep only to see a demon walking across the living room floor. It was like a fearsome wolf or a hyena, and as it walked, it stood up on its hind legs and was headed towards our bedroom. He laid there very quietly in great fear; then he coughed, and it looked and realized Bryce could see it, it began walking towards him. He was too scared to scream as he hopped off of the couch and ran into our nearby room, jumping into the middle of our bed and waking both of us up.

"What's wrong? What's going on?" Michelle asked, concerned. Our four-year-old frantically explained in little kid language the brief encounter with the scary-looking wolf demon with glowing eyes and how he ended up in our bed looking for protection and comfort.

So, I sat up and commanded, "Demon be gone in the name of Jesus."

Then I asked Bryce if it left yet. He could see it; we could not. He said, "No, it had stopped walking and was just looking at us."

I could feel this intense anger and repulsion rise up on the inside of me as I commanded it to get out of this house and never come back, in Jesus' name. "So now, what's it doing?" I asked.

"It got scared and turned and ran through the wall," our son said with great relief as he laid his head on my pillow and snuggled up to both of us safe and sound, "but the cobras are still outside the front door."

"What! You never said anything about snakes. Are they trying to come into the house?" I asked.

"Yes, but they can't come in," he answered. (I found out later that some big angel was keeping them out.) So I commanded them to leave in Jesus' name and asked, "Okay, are they still there?"

Half asleep, he looked in that direction for a moment and said, "No, they're gone," and laid his little head back on my pillow.

Our kids grew up knowing about demons and spirits and witchcraft and how to take care of them with the name of Jesus. Not because we wanted to but because we had so many unexpected experiences with them. The kids could all see the spirits, and they could also see what happened when we spoke that name against them.

When your little four-year-old is being tormented by an evil spirit he can see, and then he sees what happens when you speak the name of Jesus against it, there is no better explanation and no better teacher to show them what to do and how to deal with it.

People ask when a good time to teach your kids about this stuff is? Whenever they are ready, whatever age that may be. For us, we had no choice about when; we had to deal with things as they popped up. So the kids got to see what to do as it was happening. If they're little and they are seeing things, then they are ready regardless of whether we think they are or not. We can't forget that we have a partner in this too; we're never alone, the Holy Spirit, who helps us, and teaches us, and guides us, He's the one who knows what to do when we don't. He's the one with the answers to things we need help with, and He's the one with the power to bring the things to pass. (Of course, we need to differentiate between real and make-believe. And if they're making things up or not, especially with the younger ones.) And sometimes we need to test the spirits according to 1 John 4:1-3.

Our kids need to know the power in Jesus' name and that it really works. Just tell them in language appropriate for their age. The peace and comfort that come with the knowledge that Jesus is with them and that they have the power to stop or get rid of scary things in His name are immeasurable for them. There is something quite heartwarming when your little one tells you how they prayed and the bad thing left. By the time they are teenagers, they will have become confident about God's power to deliver them because they have actually experienced it for themselves; they have seen it happen right before their eyes.

It is written that salvation is so easy that a child can understand it. I like it that some of the other things are too. We, adults, tend to make things harder than they really are.

The Epilogue

He was dreaming and saw someone standing about twenty yards away. That person was wearing a dark cloak with the hood pulled down over his face, and his head bowed towards the ground. He looked very strong and muscular under the cloak. He just stood there, not moving, not saying a word, even when he was yelled at. Bryce walked over to him and lifted the hood. There, under the hood, was the face of the same wolf demon that had scared him when he was four. It was smiling a wicked smile, and its eyes had the same red glow. No words were spoken.

Bryce's first reaction was to reach out and grab it by the throat. When he did, the wolf demon did the same to Bryce. Unlike the incident in our living room, this time, there was no fear. They stood there looking at each other for a moment, still holding each other's throats, when Bryce pounded its face with a quick right hook and pulled loose from the throat hold. It punched back, and the fight was on. They kicked and rolled and punched each other ferociously. As the night wore on, the power and intensity of the hits kept increasing, becoming more and more devastating for each of them, to the point where it felt that each connecting blow could break a bone. It was an even match at first, but Bryce could feel he was ever so slowly getting the upper hand, blocking, punching, and kicking with a power and ferocity like he'd never felt before. The more the fight escalated, the more he could feel God's power and courage flowing through his body. He felt no weakness, and even though the fight wore on and on, he wasn't getting tired. He would fight until he won; there was no other alternative. Period!

Finally, when the punches reached an intensity that could cause death with just one blow, the wolf demon turned and ran away like it was running for its life. Bryce just stood there, victorious, watching his vanquished foe disappear into the black mist of his dream.

Suddenly reveille sounded; it was 4 a.m., time to get up. Back to the reality of fighting a war in Iraq. Sand, heat, wind, sweat, cold, explosions. Any time, anywhere, anyone on the street could be the enemy. Bryce could hardly move; he was so exhausted; his arms lay limp at his side; they were so used up and tired. He had a difficult time even getting out of bed; it was hard just to get up and get dressed. He was amazed at how weak he felt. It was then that he realized that the dream was real, and he really had spent the night fighting the wolf demon. But he won! The demon could not prevail, he had beaten it, and he had a knowing inside from the Holy Spirit that it would never be able to challenge or torment him again. That knowing felt good, really good. He was reminded of Jacobs' all-night fight with the angel and pondered what he had just been through. What else did this mean for him other than the threat from that evil spirit was done, gone forever? He felt a strong assurance and a great peace in his heart that somehow this confrontation had gotten rid of the demon and it would never come back. You know the Lord can be in our actions as well as our words, and yes, He can even be in our dreams. The Holy Spirit did the work.

Did the wolf demon attack that night because it felt there was an opening it could use against Bryce? Don't know. Was it a part of the carnage the previous day? Could have been. They had spent that morning gathering body parts from a helicopter full of marines that had been shot down right next to them.

Bryce heard it then saw the explosion. There were no survivors. The incident just served to increase everyone's resolve to take out the enemy, the terrorists who were always nearby, hurting, intimidating, and maiming the people.

The marines had captured a strategic spot and were now guarding it. A large dam where Saddam had stashed a lot of money, even gold and silver, in the middle of a barren, sandy, miserable wasteland.

All Bryce knows is that he fought for his life in his dreams, and God caused him to win against an old foe, and that old foe is never coming back. How fitting that in the middle of a combat deployment, he has a dream about hand-to-hand combat and prevails gloriously. I like that, and I like it that God doesn't do things according to the box we have Him in. Does every demonic confrontation go that way? No, this was definitely unique. But then, all of them are.

While he was deployed, we spoke Psalm 91 over him regularly. We also taught him to speak it over himself when he was little. Not only did it give us comfort, I know it helped him prevail in combat, physically, mentally, and spiritually. As a parent, you don't realize how some of the things you teach your children will actually help save their lives when they are older or even cause them to prevail in life-threatening situations. We also don't realize the power our prayers can have. All those words spoken long ago are still working for us, for our loved ones.

"So shall my word be that goeth forth out of my mouth: it shall not return unto me void, but it shall accomplish that which I please, and it shall prosper in the thing whereto I sent it" (Isaiah 55:11, KJV).

The Crows and the Grasshoppers

Grasshoppers just appeared out of nowhere one day; millions of them. They descended like a shroud of mist on every living plant and began eating them. It felt like a biblical plague of locusts. They were in everything and on everything. We couldn't get away from the clicking sound they make. The noise would rise and fall like waves of the sea rising and falling. All day and into the night. It didn't take long to figure out that this wasn't good. Parts of the meadow in front of our house were now just thin little sticks standing where healthy grass hay once stood, but with lots of dirt around it.

There wasn't a thing we could do. There were too many of them, and the area was way too big. I guess we should pray. Gosh, has it come to that? So we prayed. We said, "Lord, we don't know what to do, but we know that You do. We pray that whatever it takes to get rid of this plague that You would move and do it. We trust in You; we give this whole situation to You, and we pray that You would move even today and bring it to pass in Jesus' name."

We looked up, and nothing had happened yet.

So all throughout the day, we would stop and say, "Lord, I know You're doing something to get rid of these grasshoppers, and I know You will bring it to pass for it is written to commit our issues to You, to trust also in You, and You will bring it to pass. I thank You that Your Word is true and that You will bring this to pass. May it happen today!"

All day long, nothing seemed to be happening.

And the next day and the next.

We just kept speaking our little prayer as we thought of it and went to bed each night,

wondering what was going to happen.

On the fourth morning, we look out and see hundreds of crows just standing in the meadow and across all the land. So many of them it looked like we had planted crows in the field, and they just sprang up. Our first thought was, "Oh nuts, this is really weird." But as we watched, we realized the crows were eating the grasshoppers. They just stood in one place and ate the bugs milling around them. We watched in amazement and realized the crows were from God, and this was the answer to our prayer. The Father is pretty creative. He doesn't always answer prayer like you think it should be answered. I never know what to expect. Other than to just expect an answer, to just believe.

By evening, all the bugs were gone, and the crows, now all full and happy, flew off.

Our problem was solved, or should I say, eaten up. So what did we do? We celebrated and had locusts and honey for diner.

No, not really; we had steak with all the trimmings and praised God for answered prayer.

Slapped for the Truth

Contending for your children what's right against what's wrong can sometimes cost you something. Michelle was cleaning the car while the kids played with the neighborhood children in our front yard. As she was wiping the dashboard, she happened to look over just in time to see a larger neighbor boy grab our son right in the crotch. Shooting out of the car, she had them sit with her on the sidewalk and explained right and wrong touching until they seemed to get it. All the kids were fairly young.

The boy lived with his grandmother, and Michelle told him she was going to need to talk to her about this. He begged her almost to the point of tears not to tell because he would be in big trouble. Michelle assured him that he was not in trouble but that any time he spent with our kids had to be good and healthy and that she needed to let Grandma know what they had all discussed today and why.

Well, it turns out the boy was right. With all the kids running and jumping and playing around her, Michelle walked the three houses down the street to Grandma's house. Grandma saw them coming and came out to greet Michelle, then listened to her story of the inappropriate touching and what she had told the kids about it. Her answer to Michelle was to kick the boy as hard as she could, then command him into the house, yelling violently after him and slamming the door.

Obviously, things did not go well. Pondering what she just witnessed, Michelle walked back up the street with our boys and the rest of the neighbor kids, wondering if this situation was really over or not. Sitting on the grass, enjoying the laughter of happy children playing around her, Michelle looks up, and here comes Grandma stomping up the sidewalk towards her, huffing and puffing deep gulps of the cigarette she was smoking. Within about twenty yards of Michelle, she holds up her hand and flicks the still-burning butt into someone else's yard. The kids saw trouble coming and ran to get out of the way. Michelle called out to them, "It's okay; she's not going to hurt anyone." Little did she know the kids saw the problem long before she did.

Still stomping towards Michelle so hard her feet are slapping on the cement with every step, she begins yelling before she even gets close, "Liar, liar, you're a rotten liar," the stale cigarette smoke coming back out of the blackness of her mouth every time she opens it. Stopping, she squares off in front of Michelle, still yelling, her hot, putrid breath spewing across her face. The older lady was big, over twice Michelle's size, and big-boned too.

Michelle was shocked. She was just trying to right a wrong with the children, "I'm not lying; I was just trying to help our children play well together." Grandma refused to agree that her grandkids had done anything wrong at all, and without warning, she reached up and slapped Michelle so hard across the face it almost knocked her down as she stumbled backward, trying not to fall. Stunned, Michelle was speechless for a moment as Grandma moved in and started pounding her pointed finger so hard into Michelle's chest that it hurt and was knocking her backward with each hit. Determined now to stand her ground and protect herself, Michelle began yelling, "Don't you touch me again." But Grandma just attacked more ferociously. Finally, during a split second where Grandma had to take a breath, Michelle pointed her finger at her and roared with all the intensity that had built up inside her, "I rebuke you in the name of Jesus!" Instantly it was like an unseen force smacked Grandma backward onto the grass on the other side of the sidewalk. Everyone was astonished, Michelle, all the neighborhood kids, and especially the nasty grandma. Then Michelle thrust the palm of her hand out towards her and said with great power and intensity, "You will not touch me or my children ever again, in Jesus' name!"

"Greater is he that is in you, than he that is in the world" (1 John 4:4, KJV).

The wicked old woman was now pacing back and forth like a rabid wolf at the invisible line that she could not cross, taunting Michelle with every profane and vile thing she could think of. But what's amazing is that once she had been knocked into the grass on the other side of the sidewalk, she was actually unable to take a step back onto it. It was like some spiritual force kept her there and wouldn't let her even one inch closer to Michelle. Seeing she couldn't get close to intimidate Michelle anymore, she got down on her knees, holding her arms out in mock worship, bowing all the way to the ground then up into the air over and over again while she said mockingly, "You think you're holy, oh you're so holy, you think you're so holy," over and over again.

"Come, let's go home now." Our kids carefully took a wide berth around the wicked grandma, looking at her with disgust and wonder as they took Michelle's hands and walked back across the street. As they went calmly home, no one looked back; they just ignored her, stepped into the house, and shut the door. Grandma was still on her knees the whole time, bowing up and down, mocking them and spewing vile and vulgar things out of her mouth, the neighborhood kids nearby hearing everything and watching in amazement as this all unfolded in front of them.

> This book of the law shall not depart from your mouth, but you shall meditate on it day and night... for then you will make your way prosperous, and then you will achieve success...Be strong and courageous! Do not terrified nor dismayed, for the Lord your God is with you wherever you go.
>
> Joshua 1:8-9

Once inside, Michelle decided to call the police and report her. The wicked grandma told the cops she had done nothing wrong and didn't even know what we were talking about. After speaking to our family, they charged her with assault and battery, then lowered the charge, fined her, put her on short probation, and slapped a restraining order against her not to come near any of us again. Because she's a grandma, a good actor, and an incredibly good liar, the police and the judge had pity on her and didn't do what they could have done. But we were satisfied.

Immediately afterward, her son, in his late thirties (his children are the ones Michelle had to speak to about inappropriate touching), would pull up in front of our house, roll down his window, rev his engine and threaten Michelle, then squeal off. You could see into our front door because it was usually open to help cool the house in the heat of summer. He was trying to intimidate her, but she wouldn't have it. Every time he'd pull up and start his show, she would step into the open doorway and rebuke Satan and anything he would try to do and any assignment against our family. Every time she would rebuke Satan in Jesus' name, the guy would quickly leave. When he saw that Michelle couldn't be intimidated, he stopped coming by.

"I will be with him in trouble, and I will rescue him" (Psalm 91:15).

He would never come by when I was home. Coward! I wanted so badly to deal with this in my own strength. I really didn't want to forgive them, I wanted to be mad, and I wanted to personally stop the son from trying to intimidate my wife. That really grated on me, but it was not for me to do. My wife and the Lord both made it clear that it would only do more harm than good and that it was also a spiritual matter.

"Not by might, nor by power but by my Spirit says the Lord Almighty" (Zechariah 4:6, NIV).

I had to be reminded that God is bigger than this and has the power to take care of it better than I can, and His way has no bad repercussions. Look how He had just delivered Michelle. So, I forgave them to loose myself from them; I also had to ask the Lord to remove the hatred I felt, it was only hurting me, and I spoke certain scriptures over the situation, and it quickly changed. Imagine that. My mind was no longer in turmoil over things; peace replaced that, and the need to vindicate my wife left my thinking. Within a short time, the people and the issues just melted away. Even though they lived just down the street, it was as if they totally disappeared. What a relief!

No matter how big the mess, the Lord can change things and deliver us.

Psalm 59, this is a wonderful psalm for threatening and difficult situations.

Little Boy Lost His Puppy

A lady called from Alaska. Her grandson had lost his puppy, and she wanted prayer so that maybe the Lord would bring it back. They had gone for a day to the beach. It was a wildly rugged and beautiful place without sand, just rocks. The weather was pleasant enough for a picnic, which they enjoyed near the cold, crashing waves that sprayed mightily upward and made little rainbows in the sunlight. The grandson was five, and the puppy, about twelve weeks. All day long, they had played and run run run together. Over the rocks, around the rocks, in the water, then back to the forest that nestled up to the beach of stones. Now tired, they laid on top of each other, squirming around to get comfortable on the smooth rocks, enjoying the last bit of warmth of the setting sun and catching their breath.

Suddenly, the puppy heard a noise that demanded his attention. Jerking his head up, he raised his little ears while peering off into the forest, trying to perceive more about the mystery noise. Then without warning, he took off as fast as his puppy legs would take him, jumping, slipping, running, and falling across the rocks towards the trees. The whole family yelled at him in vain to stop or come back or whatever. You know how it is when everyone is speaking, and no one knows what anyone else is saying; it's just a jumble of voices. I'm sure the puppy thought the same thing. But he didn't care. He was a puppy on a mission. And with that, he disappeared into the dark of the forest, his bark fading until there was no sound but the soft summer breeze through the branches of the trees and the surf pounding far behind them.

They searched until way after dark. But no Puppy (that was his name for now). Sadly, they still had a three-hour drive home, and there was no way to come back to look anymore. It seemed the puppy was now lost forever—what a terrible predicament. Unfazed, the little boy boldly proclaimed, "Jesus will bring my puppy back. He will bring him to the sheriff, and the sheriff will bring him to me. Let's pray for him." So he bowed his little head, put his hands together, and prayed a short little prayer for Puppy that only a child could pray. The family all voiced "Amen" together to show their support, though none of them believed the prayer, not even Grandma, the rock of faith in the family. Lifting his head, his eyes sparkling with hope, the little boy said, "Don't worry, Jesus will help us now."

His words pierced Grandma's heart, and his simple faith jolted her unbelief. He was actually living and practicing what Jesus told Jairus to do, "Just believe." How easy she thought to herself, yet also so hard. She didn't know if she could really believe that things would happen according to her grandson's prayer, but she wanted them to, she wanted to believe. Still struggling with what she believed and what she didn't believe, she called us and asked for prayer after a sleepless night.

The prayer was simple "Lord God, we agree with everything the little boy prayed, and we stand in faith like You said to do and believe that it will come to pass, and the puppy will be brought home in Jesus' name." Still struggling, Grandma was encouraged to stand according to another scripture: "Lord, I believe yet help my unbelief" (Mark 9:24, NKJV).

Grandma determined to stand that day to the best of her ability in agreement with her grandsons' prayer. The battle in her mind was great, but she would always go back to our prayer together and repeat it to herself and then move on with her day. Even though sometimes it felt like she had to do this every five minutes, she was determined. Determined to stand and see something hopefully come to pass, though she didn't know how or when.

The next morning the little boy ran to the end of the driveway and looked expectantly up and down the beautiful, tree-lined country road they lived on, hoping to see either puppy or the sheriff. But there was nothing, no dog and no sheriff. Undeterred, he slowly walked back to the house, mumbling something about Jesus and Puppy. This happened every hour for the rest of the day and the next day, and the next. Soon the week was over with no word about Puppy. Grandma was really struggling with what to believe now, and the rest of the family had begun saying things they hoped would make the situation easier on the little boy if nothing happened and Puppy never came home.

They didn't want to discourage him, but they also wanted him to be practical about things and not be hurt if his prayer wasn't answered. They were all Christians, they all believed prayer works, they also knew sometimes things don't always happen the way you prayed for them.

Another week went by. The little boy kept up his ritual of checking the road every hour or so to see if his prayer was answered yet, and the rest of the family were frantic and trying not to show it to him. They couldn't stand the thought of unanswered prayer and the pain that would follow. How would they help him cope?

What would it do to his faith, what would it do to his belief in God? This faith thing was getting out of hand. What should they do now? What should they say?

Despite often getting caught up in the total impossibility of the situation with the rest of the family, Grandma always had this faint glimmer of hope deep inside that wouldn't go away, and it helped her to continue to believe that something might happen. She beat herself up for constantly wavering in her faith. This had to be one of the hardest seasons of faith she had ever had in her long life, and it wasn't even over yet.

Another long, painful week was coming to a close. The whole family was feeling like a basket case, reeling with all the imaginations of what might happen and knowing for certain that Puppy had been eaten by some wild animal. Yet, in all that, the little boy never wavered in his belief that Jesus was going to help them.

It was dusk, the sun had set, but its warm light filled the sky when a pickup pulled into the yard and parked where the grass would have been if they had had a lawn. A jolly, weathered man in a cowboy hat with something under his arm bounced up to the front door. His powerful knocks popped the solid wooden door wide open. Beaming from ear to ear, he bellowed, "I have something I believe belongs to a certain young man in this house" There, squirming under the arm of the big man, was Puppy. For a moment, time stood still. No one could move; everyone was in shocked amazement. The sheriff bent over and launched Puppy on the floor as the little boy dove for the dog, wrapping him in his arms while his little friend excitedly licked the tears streaming down the boy's face.

Grandma called later that weekend to tell us the good news of answered prayer.

No one knew how the sheriff got the dog; in the excitement, they never thought to ask. Puppy did have a tag on his little collar. They only know it happened and that he is a man and not an angel. Though if you ask the little boy, he may give a different answer. This family is forever changed and will never again doubt the faith of a little boy or that God answers prayer.

This all happened when I worked at the prayer center of a large ministry. I was blessed to have a part in praying for this situation.

The Pool of Wisdom

May you grow in the Lord
and become that refreshing pool of wisdom,
so that others may come to you,
and dip from you,
and get the answers
and the revelation
they are looking for.

Jesus in Tahiti

We took our honeymoon in Tahiti. Wow, what a tropical paradise. We left a snowstorm in Colorado, and eighteen hours later, we were watching some young guys with shorts and no shirts guide our plane over the tarmac. We spent a couple of nights on the island of Tahiti and took a romantic, madly-in-love, honeymoon-ish drive exploring the place, looking at the waterfalls, wandering through the jungle, the beach, and all the incredible scenery. One waterfall was so magnificent, so powerful, that the wind it created where it thundered into a hidden jungle pool blew our hair straight backward and was so full of moisture that we were soaking wet in seconds. We watched awestruck at the beauty, the sound, and the power for a while; we'd never seen anything like this before and tried to take it all in before we sloshed happily back on the jungle trail to our topless car.

All the Tahitian women wear these colorful sheet-looking things called "muumuus." It's very feminine and really fits the mystique of the islands and the tropics.

They also pick from all the beautiful flowers that grow everywhere, I mean everywhere, and put them in their hair. At our first hotel, Michelle found a muumuu tying class and went. She found out twenty ways to tie those things, and most of them looked good. She liked them so much, and they were so comfortable that that is all she wore for much of the trip. I liked it; she always tied them in a way that looked good on her. An I'm on my honeymoon sort of good. Following the island example, she also put flowers all through her hair.

Next was a week on Bora Bora which became our favorite spot. At the front desk, the manager from Nebraska who'd lived there for years, bantered with a six-foot-tall, 250-pound Tahitian woman with her long dark hair wound into a tight knot on top of her huge head. "Hey, big mama, carry these good folks to their hut." We had piled our heavy bags in the middle of the floor with all the other baggage. She put her hand over her mouth, giggled girlishly, then easily picked them all up, threw the smaller ones under her arms, and took off like a freight train on a mission. Wide-eyed, we looked at each other, laughed, and followed her off into the wild green yonder, down winding paths of jungle and flowers to our thatched hut in the palm trees by the sea.

We snorkeled for hours in the crystal-clear lagoon filled with coral and life and colors and odd and mysterious things we'd never seen before. We frolicked, played, and picnicked, paddled our outrigger into the night, and explored love and the island for the whole glorious week. Every evening we would sit enjoying the tropical warmth and watch the sunset, then go and eat a delicious dinner. We actually saw the "green flash" about five or six times. Incredible! I didn't realize it, but I guess some folks have looked for it all their lives and never seen it, and here we see it almost every night for a week. I think we were blessed. It happens at the exact moment when the sun dips beneath the ocean on the horizon, and this green flash shoots up into the sky. If you blink, you might miss it. It looks like something supernatural is happening.

Author snorkeling in Bora Bora

The dining was always an excellent adventure. All meals were served by the local Tahitian women in a very comfortable large, thatched building on huge, thick, tree stump stilts overlooking the water. We always sat where we could look out over the calm, pristine lagoon, the muted sound of waves thundering about 400 yards away as they crash against the reef encircling the island, and beyond that, the immense span of ocean that stretched on until it disappeared at the edge of the world. We spent long romantic hours savoring every minute, or should I say, bite of each meal.

Sometimes we took the little golf cart like cars and explored the island, which didn't take long but was always fun. What isn't fun when you're in love? Especially in a tropical paradise. Everywhere we went on all the islands, we found incredible views, exotic smells, mysterious forest paths, beautiful beaches, hidden streams, and crystal-clear pools, odd plants, and fruit growing wild in the strangest of places. Tahitians fishing with harpoons or nets just as their ancestors had, and of course, the flowers everywhere growing on everything. Sometimes on the road by the jungle, we would hear an overwhelming hum. Overwhelming because it was so loud and continuous that it was weirdly bothersome, like the jungle was alive with something. Come to find out, it was insects making all those noises. Now that's a lot of bugs!

Then off to Moorea. The simple yet well-appointed lobby was empty; no one was at the front desk. It felt eerie. We were the only ones checking in, and no matter how loud we yelled, no one answered. After a long time, a clerk showed up unhurried, obviously on Tahitian time, and showed us to our hut.

An odd-looking man with a large Panama hat was just outside our door under a small tree with red flowers and leaves like dinner plates. He was raking something, slowly, so very slowly that it caught our attention. He kept making the exact same motion in the exact same spot like he was a robot stuck in place. The clerk didn't look at him or even acknowledge him; he wouldn't look up at us as we went by. Setting our luggage down, Michelle pointed him out and how weird he made her feel. Looking at each other, then over towards him again, but he wasn't there. What! How could he have disappeared so quickly?

Now we were really bothered; something just wasn't right here. Everything about that guy felt weird in almost a dangerous kind of way.

And what's worse, at least for Michelle, is that the geckos in the bathroom weren't afraid of her. They just stuck their little selves right there on the wall and calmly turned their heads and rolled their eyes and watched her every time she came in. Can't a girl have her privacy? You could shoo them away, but they always returned. They seemed to enjoy Michelle a lot; I think she was their entertainment.

Later that evening, we finally saw some other people at dinner. By the conversations around us, we could tell we were the only Americans. The food was again quite good, but the two-foot-long coconut rat was a bit bothersome. Have you ever seen a two-foot rat? Being chased out of the kitchen by a determined cook with a broom swinging wildly as it scurried from under one table to the next, trying to hide. His claws were clacking and scraping on the slick red tile floor as he ran frantically to get away. You should have seen the women shrieking and screaming in all their different languages and going through all types of contortions to avoid him as he darted like a ping pong ball from table to table, even running over some of their feet and sliding under just about every table in the dining room. Then, sure enough, here he came running straight for us. I mean running! If a rat could have panic on his face, this one sure did. I was sure those beady little eyes were opened in fear about twice as wide as normal. Without any hesitation, he darted under our table; I lifted my feet as he sped under them, then headed on out into the safety of the night. There were no walls around the dining area, just a thatched roof over it all, with the kitchen area in the middle and a wooden railing around the perimeter. We looked at our food and wondered if we should eat any more. Heck yaa! We weren't going to let some stupid rat ruin our evening.

The next day we rented a motorcycle to tour the island. Okay, so it was a mini moto and not a real motorcycle. This island was bigger than Bora Bora, and there was a lot to see.

We were on this dirt road that had been flat and easy for a long way. All was well until the road started to go straight up the side of the mountain in the middle of the island. I had to downshift to keep going. Only one problem, I'd never ridden a motorcycle before, and downshifting without really knowing what you're doing isn't that easy. I put it off as long as I could, but now the mini moto was sputtering along, going so slow, we were going to tip over sidewards if I didn't just do it. When I had tried it before, it ground the gears pretty bad and sounded like it might explode, so I was a little shy about trying it again.

Michelle, of course, didn't know how much I didn't know. But that didn't matter because I figured I could figure it out. I held in the clutch, put the gear lever down with my foot, and thought I had done it. Yea! So I popped the clutch and Boosh! The thing took on a life of its own, shooting straight up in the air. I hung on for dear life to keep it from going over my head backward on Michelle. I still had the handles in my hands and was standing on the dirt because the darn thing had shot out from between my legs and was wildly trying to go out somewhere if I'd just let go, which I wouldn't, and then it just stopped, and I let it fall out of the air onto its side.

Taking in what just happened, I hear behind me, "Well, I'm never riding on that thing with you again!" And, turning around, there's Michelle flat on her back in the dirt, laying right where she'd been thrown when the mini moto shot up into the air. I laughed because the situation was funny, and I could see she wasn't hurt, laying there on her back in the middle of the road, her cute little orange muumuu, her beautiful blond hair sticking out from her head like the rays of the sun, dust all over both of us—big mistake for a newlywed guy, the laughing part that is.

Then just like he was right on cue, a great big Tahitian with long, thick, black, windblown hair sticking out in every direction came by on his own little mini moto and saw we needed help. When it had crashed to the ground, it quit running, and I couldn't get it started again. His Tahiti mama sat smiling, looking quite amused by us and our predicament. "You speak French?" he asked.

"No. Do you speak English?" I responded.

"No." He fumbled with the bike awhile and vroom; it started right up.

"*Merci beaucoup*," I said, thankful for his help and showing off the French I do know. Michelle added, "*Mauru' uru*," which means "thank you" in Tahitian. It's a bit of a mouthful of a word, but the natives loved it when she said it to them. Smiling one of those huge, big man happy smiles, he turned it back over to us and mounted his tiny motorbike and scooted off. Just the picture of this huge, broad-shouldered man on that tiny mini moto disappearing in the distance with Tahiti mama holding on tight behind him was hilarious.

Convincing Michelle to get back on the thing and ride with me around the island took a while, but she finally agreed. Dusting each other off and picking the various pieces of road dirt and jungle out of our hair, we got back on the bike. Determined to conquer the ole mini moto, I gave it some gas, and off we go. So it was only five miles an hour; we were moving off again on our adventure. Sure enough, after a while, I had to downshift again before we quit moving and fell over. Taking a deep breath, I yelled, "Okay, hold on tight; I'm going to shift."

"Great," she responded facetiously, holding on tighter just in case it didn't work. You know what? It worked this time, and every time afterward, I finally got it figured out.

On top of the mountain in the middle of the island, the view is stunning. Tropical paradise everywhere you look. A crystal blue lagoon surrounded a lush emerald green landscape peppered with every colored flower growing wild everywhere you look. Taking it in for a long time, we then rode down to the other side. I had seen something on a map about an old religious spot that still had its altar beside the road, so I searched until we found it.

We had to walk a little way through the jungle to get to it, but it wasn't hard to find. By the look of the path, I could tell this wasn't a well-visited place. Expecting maybe an old church or something, we were surprised to find a large area paved with flat hand-hewn stones slick with moss. A mound about eight feet long, three feet wide, and three feet high of carefully stacked stones was at the far end. Looking at them, I could tell they had made up the altar long ago, and it had fallen apart some in the many years since it had been used. This was an ancient native place—a place where they had performed their pagan ceremonies and practiced human sacrifice. Before the Europeans showed up, they had been cannibals. It had a weird, icky, scary, slimy, even dangerous feel to it. It almost sounded like you could hear voices from the past crying out from the stones and the thick jungle around us. Michelle became so uneasy she couldn't stay any longer and bolted back to the road. Taking a last look around before I left, it felt like there was something evil looking back at me from the dense jungle ringing this place of ancient death. We also noticed that the jungle immediately around the stones looked like it was poisoned, always dying; nothing could grow there. It was weird and unnerving, so we quickly hopped back on the mini moto and sped away.

After dinner in the Coconut Rat Restaurant, we laid on top of our bed, looking into the darkness of the thatched roof above us, enjoying the breeze created by the large ceiling fan constantly rotating between the rafters. The annoying, screeching night birds had started up. Sometimes they were so loud we could hardly sleep. They didn't just screech; they sometimes screamed; it was terrible, actually tormenting. Amazingly everyone we asked about them said they had never heard them. How could anyone else not hear that noise? It was so loud! Then we found out they were spirits, screaming spirits, which was very unnerving; we didn't know that Christians could hear spirits screaming like that, and we definitely had no clue what to do about it. We were hearing things in the spirit realm, and the other folks weren't; that's why they had no clue what we were talking about. They just thought we were a bit weird. I don't blame them for thinking that. I would've thought the same thing if I hadn't heard it for myself.

About then, something big hit the fan and fell with a big plop right on the sheet on top of Michelle's foot. She heard it hit the fan and felt it hit the bed. She saw it lying there in the dark and screamed, kicking her feet wildly to get it off. It was black and as big as a bread and butter plate, and when she kicked, we heard it smack against the side of the hut near the door. Jumping out of bed, she quickly turned on the light and...

Nothing was there. Whatever it was, it got away. So, was it still in our room? Was it on the floor or under the bed? Looking around the room, we couldn't find anything. What the heck was it? She didn't know if she could go to sleep, knowing that this big mysterious black thing might still be in the hut crawling around, maybe even back on our bed. It was a bit unsettling until I decided not to be afraid of it and go to sleep; she eventually dozed off too without any more weirdness falling out of the thatched roof onto our bed.

Feeling the hands close tightly around my neck while I was in that place between asleep and awake, I suddenly couldn't breathe. Thrashing wildly and fighting against it, I tried in vain to get loose. I felt like I was dying. I couldn't get away, and I couldn't take a breath, then it lifted me up off of my knees off of the bed into the air and squeezed tighter. At first, I thought I was dreaming, but then I realized I wasn't, that this was real, and it got very scary. I pulled helplessly at the invisible fingers squeezing my neck. I couldn't feel them with my hands, but I could feel them around my throat. The noise and commotion woke Michelle up; she watched in astonishment at what was happening, and without even hesitating, the words screamed up and out from the depths of her being, "Jesus! Jesus! Jesus!"

Instantly whatever it was, threw me violently down onto the bed, I landed flat on my back. The fingers gripping my throat were gone, and I felt so exhausted I could hardly move. "Whoa! What was that all about?" I just laid there motionless and breathing deeply until I got my breath back, trying to process what had just happened. It was the night of our visit to the ancient native sacrificial altar. Somehow, we both knew that had something to do with it. It was an unseen spirit, and it was trying to kill me. But why? How could it do that? The name of Jesus at least made it stop and got rid of it. Thank God for the power in the name of Jesus. Thank God Michelle knew to say it; who knows what might have happened to me if she didn't. And on our honeymoon, for Pete's sake.

This was our first experience with spirits and the name of Jesus. Michelle said she heard strongly in her heart, "Say the name of Jesus, say the name of Jesus." So she did, and it sure worked well. I was set free from some spirit trying to kill me in my own bed. How could it do that? Nothing like this had ever happened to me before. We definitely needed to know more about this spirit stuff. So begins a wonderful, lifelong journey together into the things of God and the things of the Spirit.

She Walks in Beauty

Yes, she walks in beauty;
it's there for all to see;
her grace, her form, her loveliness,
her femininity.

Her tongue is touched with wisdom;
her answers good and true;
give strength and love, encouragement,
life and hope renewed.

Her love is like a flower
that blooms new every day;
more colors, fragrance, passion, sweet;
a beautiful bouquet.

Her children rise and call her blessed
as they walk through life and grow;
her love the fabric clothing them
everywhere they go.

Her future always one of hope;
her faith is ever new
words, thoughts, dreams fulfilled
her God is ever true.

Yes, she walks in beauty;
it's there for all to see;
her grace, her form, her loveliness;
God's special gift to me.

49

Witches in Boulder

We were out for a date night. I had wanted to take Michelle to dinner at this special restaurant in Boulder for some time, and now here we were. We got a babysitter for the kids, dressed up nice, and we were looking forward to a wonderful and relaxing experience together without any interruptions.

We were seated at a good table in a smaller and more intimate area. Perfect for our anniversary meal. Looking around, I saw all the tables were occupied with content and happy people, and the smell of good food filled the air—what a nice atmosphere. Even the waitress was attentive without being annoying. The appetizer we shared was delicious; we wanted to save room for the rest of the meal, so we ordered just one. Savoring the last bite before the real meal came, I looked down the aisle at the rest of the tables in the room.

Did I really just see that? Did that really just happen? Here? While we are eating dinner?

Just two tables away was a couple at a four-top seated in the chairs by the aisle. The man was facing me, and the lady had her back to us. He had this goofy look on his face and started laughing very derisively in our direction while the lady turned her head to look directly at us. But that's the thing. She turned only her head while her body stayed facing the other direction, just like in some horror movie. Her eyes were unnaturally black, and she mouthed some unintelligible words, then turned back around to face the guy. All without moving her body. Wow, that was weird; how'd she do that anyway? Seeing the odd look on my face Michelle turned to see what I was looking at, and when she did, the lady turned around again, her head moved all the way around backward, and her body stayed facing the other way. That's not possible! How did she do that without breaking her neck? Something isn't right with that.

We are used to weirdness in Boulder. One time walking down Pearl Street, there was a man dancing to drums. He was dancing with all his might, sweating profusely, but he went on and on and on, and he was speaking a language we didn't understand as he went through his wild gyrations. All of a sudden, he said something we could understand; we both heard it. It sounded like it came out of the other language; I don't know how else to explain it. And he said this, "Please help me I want to be free, I want to be free, please help me I am a prisoner please help me, I can't stop, I can't stop, I can't stop." as he continued dancing.

We were newly married, new Christians, and we didn't know what to do or what to even think about that. We'd never seen nor heard of anything like this before, so we just walked off. After a few steps, we both felt so convicted in our hearts to do something that we turned around and went back and just stood there because we didn't know what else to do. We finally felt that we should pray for him to be set free in the name of Jesus. So we did, quietly from a distance. Nothing appeared to happen, but we felt a peace that we had prayed the right thing, so we went on about our day. We still don't know what happened to that guy; I guess we'll find out when we get to heaven.

But I digress.

Now a few years later, we'd heard of other people's experiences dealing with the occult but still didn't know how to handle things ourselves. Feeling concerned and angry that this was interfering with our diner, I looked at Michelle and said, "Now, what do we do?"

"I think we should pray," she said uneasily.

"Oh, okay," I said and looked directly at them and prayed something, but I have no clue what. Then we waited a few very long, unnerving minutes, and absolutely nothing happened, and we felt more agitated and worse. Well, that sure worked well. Now what? Then I felt very strongly to pray in the Spirit. Here? In the middle of this busy restaurant? Now?

After discussing it, we decided to hold hands across the table and do it as quietly as possible. Which was a great relief for me as I hadn't thought I could do it like that, (quietly that is). As we prayed, we quickly felt the fear leave us, but we were still bothered. Not as bothered as the witch couple, though. They were squirming like they had ants in their pants, their eyes were kind of bugged out, and they were making strange noises. I mean really strange noises. Everyone in our area had stopped eating and was looking at them. Pretty soon, they stood up and literally bolted out of the restaurant without looking back. I didn't even see them pay their bill.

Amazed, we stopped and looked at each other just in time for the main course to show up. It was excellent, of course.

We basked in the peace that had fallen upon us and ate every last bite with joy over our victory. What an interesting night this turned out to be. Who would have thought that praying in the Spirit would not only stop the witchcraft but get rid of the witches, too? This turned out to be a foundational revelation for us in dealing successfully with the many things that were to come.

Hundreds of Dolphins

Our good friends Oak and Oakette had arranged for us to take a boat out to watch dolphins. It was used for research during the week and took fish watchers out on weekends. They had told Oakette when she booked the trip that there hadn't been many dolphin sightings lately, and when they did see them, there weren't very many. So I just prayed as we were driving there, "Lord, I pray that You would bring a bunch of dolphins for us to see. As a matter of fact, how about so many that even the boat people haven't ever seen that many at once before, in Jesus' name." Then I thought to myself, *I know You can do this, Father, and I sure hope that You do.*

We boarded the boat with about thirty other people. We were scattered around on the main deck and an upper deck. The sun was shining, it was a beautiful day, and we were headed straight out to sea. I like standing at the very front of the boat watching as we slice through the waves, heaving and falling as we go over them. I like the wind in my face, the salt spray, the smell of the ocean, and to see what I can see.

Suddenly someone cries out, "There they are." We all look in every direction to find them. Off in the distance on the port side of the boat, we could see them jumping and surfacing and blowing water in the air as they breathed. Not much later, I could see them racing just under the water near the boat. I watched for a long time, mesmerized by how fascinating they looked almost under my feet in the water below.

Snapping out of my trance, I look out, and they are everywhere, jumping in two's and five's and even twelves, splashing gracefully back into the water then jumping again. The sea was literally so alive with dolphins that it felt like we were in the middle of a cartoon. The crew started commenting how they had never seen so many dolphins all at once. There were hundreds of them on every side.

Our friends reminded me of my prayer, and we thought about how God is interested in the things we are interested in. Even the small, seemingly unimportant things. In 1 Timothy 6:17, it says that He richly supplies us with all things to enjoy. Well, I have to say we sure enjoyed the dolphins today. Thanks, Father.

Mountain Lion Under the House

I got the call after dark; Brian needed help with a special situation the next morning. I prepare for work with him by praying in the Spirit until I feel I'm done because it's always more than a situation, it's an adventure, and I need to be ready for anything. You never know what you're getting into with Brian.

It was a modern house sitting on top of a shoulder of the mountain, up a canyon from Boulder. No real view because it was surrounded by trees, though you could see down into the ravine below, it was beautiful inside, with large windows and hardwood finishes throughout. We had lost count climbing up about one hundred steps just to get to the front door. We parked in a little wide spot off the dirt road where the owner parks. He said they brought their groceries and other things up and down the stairs, it was incredibly inconvenient, but they said they loved living there. They refused to park on what looked like a nice but overgrown driveway because they said they didn't want to ruin the natural habitat. Looking out at the driveway again, I saw that there was a really thick, tall, healthy crop of weeds that had choked out any naturally occurring vegetation. Hmmm.

We were called because they knew there was a lion living under the house, and they were afraid he had killed something and left it there to rot. They wanted us to find it and remove it. The smell of rotting flesh was overwhelming throughout the entire home; in some rooms, it was so strong that it almost made you feel like vomiting. Actually, it was so bad I had to work to control my gag reflex.

He said they had noticed the smell a couple of weeks ago but that only recently it had become unbearable. Ya think? My friend Brian the trapper and killer of all pests, large and small, always called when he had a difficult situation he needed help with. He didn't know what he was getting into with this one and wanted help if he really did need to trap a mountain lion.

I asked the homeowner why he let a mountain lion, a potentially dangerous predator, live under their house. He was convinced he was helping the balance of life somehow and welcomed anything that wanted to live there. Somehow, he thought all the animals could live in harmony under his roof. That somehow, it would help the karma in the neighborhood. Except that four or five of the neighbors' dogs had disappeared recently along with numerous cats and then the raccoon they usually left food out for on the deck hadn't been around for a month, and now he was starting to wonder if he'd maybe upset the balance of life and could be held responsible for these tragic deaths. They're from Boulder; what else do I need to say.

Going around to the back of the house, I noticed there was a large opening in the cement foundation the size of a double-car garage door. It looked like the mouth of a large cave. He pointed into the dark and said, "That's where he lives."

"Is he here now?" I asked. He didn't know. Taking our flashlights, we scanned the interior as far as we could see, which wasn't very far. The ceiling of the cave was the bottom of the floor above us, about eight feet high. Mounds of dirt that had never been removed during the building of the home filled the area. We could walk in about ten feet or so; then the dirt rose up to just below the floor joists everywhere except a couple of areas where we could crawl on hands and knees to where we could see the fifty feet or so to the back wall.

We decided not to go back there and made a lot of noise and pounded on things to disturb the big cat, so if he was in there, he'd want to leave. Then we went back upstairs to allow him to escape without being in his way.

Heading back down and hoping he was now gone (they usually don't stay anywhere people are unless somethings wrong with them), we crawled as far back as we could without getting on our stomachs and found the scattered remains of some of the dogs, cats, deer and yes, the raccoon. We could tell what they were by the tufts of fur that remained with the dried-up skin on the bones. The smell was almost overwhelming. We were relieved; we had found the source of the problem, we thought. They better be paying a lot for us to remove all these dead, rotting, mostly eaten animals.

Moving farther towards the back of the lion's den, we carefully made our way, constantly looking for any sign of a lion. Suddenly Brian cries out, "There he is!" I couldn't see from my angle, so crawling over a hump of dirt to where he is, I look at where the flashlight is shining, and sure enough, barely visible through the tiny crack was the blond fur we were looking for, showing between the floor joist and the dirt piled up almost to it. I threw a dirt clod at it, and it broke right in the crack. No movement. Hmmm...now what? A few more dirt clods shattering by him, and still, nothing happened. He was sure controlling himself and staying still. What's wrong with this lion? Why doesn't he just dart out of here? Sure, it would make it easier on me.

I wonder if he's waiting for us to leave so he can go, too. So again, we go upstairs into the disgusting-smelling house to wait and give him some time to get out.

Five minutes later, we're back down in the lion's den, looking to see if we can still see him. Yep, sure can. Well, nuts, now what?

Crawling back out to the opening, we're both surprised to see there's another guy standing there, a forest ranger. And what? The fire chief from the volunteer fire department. What're they doing here? we wondered. So we ask them. The forest ranger had been called by the homeowner, and he, in turn, had called the fire chief for backup if necessary.

"We're getting quite the entourage down here," I said to Brian.

"Ya," he responded, "I had no clue any of these people were coming."

It was getting colder outside; snow was beginning to fall lightly around us as a storm was moving in. Not wanting an audience of looky-loos, especially from Boulder judging everything we were doing. I tried to hand my flashlight to the ranger.

"Here, you go get him."

"No way," he almost yelled, looking shocked that I would offer it to him. "He might kill me; no, I'm here to offer backup for you if you need help," he said as he patted the pistol on his hip.

"Oh, that's comforting," I answered. "I have a whole support team here to watch me get torn to pieces by a cornered lion. That really makes me feel good." I taunted back. Then, looking at the chief, I said, "Here, how about you?" as I motioned for him to take the flashlight and go after the lion. Quickly pulling his hands back so I couldn't put it in them, he explained that he was here in case I got stuck or needed medical attention. Chuckling to myself, I thought, *What the heck did I let Brian get me into this time?*

The ranger had brought a catch pole, which is a pole with a noose on the end of it used to catch animals. While holding it out to me, the ranger says, "Hey, I brought this for you so that when you get close enough, you can get it around his head and hopefully control him and keep him from hurting you. See, this is how you adjust the noose to get it around his neck." Well, that part was easier than I thought, and the pole was about four feet long. He also had a rope that they tied to my ankle. That way, if anything happened and I couldn't get myself out, they thought they could pull me out with the rope. How comforting.

Now how to get back to where we had seen him. The only way was between the joists on top of the dirt. I didn't like the look of it. It looked like it would be the same as crawling in a tight tunnel on your belly. Searching the darkness with the light, I could see down the path but couldn't see any lion, no eyes reflecting back at me, nothing. And I was right. It was going to be tight. No way Brian could make it; he was six feet three inches and at least 250 and big-boned. He could hardly get his big ole head up in the hole. Me, I don't have that problem; I'm 165 and five feet nine inches.

It was easy at first, crawling on my hands and knees, but then it quickly got harder. I had to lay on my stomach and pull myself along. Stretching my arms out in front of me and pulling until my elbows hit the joists beside me and at the same time pushing with the toes of my shoes. I couldn't bend my knees; it was too narrow and tight. This moved me about six inches each time, all the while holding the catch pole in one hand the flashlight in the other. After a couple of feet, I thought, *Man, this is going to be tedious,* plus having my hands full wasn't helping any.

Getting my bearings, I shined the light forward as far as I could see; there was still no lion, nothing but blackness. But there was an abundance of spider webs I would have to go through, and as I looked closely, many had live spiders in them. Great, I hate spiders. Laying there looking at all the webs and thinking about it, I turned my hat around backward, so the bill was over my bare neck; I figured that way, if a spider dropped down, at least it wouldn't be going down my shirt. *Yuk!* I cringed at every web I pushed through until my focus returned to my mission as I was reminded, I would probably soon run face to face with a lion, and I had to be sharply aware and ready.

The passageway was now so tight that if I lowered my head, it put my face in the dirt, and I couldn't raise it above the level of my back, or I'd bump into the bottom of the floor above me. So I had to hold my head at an angle and kind of look out through my eyebrows to see forward. Not very comfortable, I might add.

It was so cramped, plus thinking about all the spiders again, that I realized I was starting to hyperventilate, and I could feel fear coming upon me. "No in the name of Jesus, no." I was speaking strongly with great conviction, "No, no, no! I don't accept this; I do not have the spirit of fear but love power and a sound mind. I have a sound mind in Jesus' name! I have a sound mind in Jesus' name! I have a sound mind in Jesus' name! I have a sound mind! I can do this; I can do this!" The seconds seemed like hours, but finally, I felt peace wrap around me. The tension just floated out of my body and my mind; what an incredible feeling of relief. It was my sign that I was okay now.

"What are you saying?" they yelled from far behind me.

"Oh, nothing, just talking to myself."

"Are you okay?" they asked.

"Ya, I am now; was starting to get a little claustrophobic, but I'm okay now, I'm over it."

"See anything yet?"

"Nope, not yet. There's no way that big ole cat got in this way, especially dragging his kills with him. He came in a different way."

I reached and felt the back of my neck under my hat to see if any spiders had fallen on me. Nope, no spiders. It was just a little distracting to move forward to face a lion, thinking there might be spiders crawling down my neck and into my shirt. Thank God there weren't any on me! Now I could move on.

It stayed this way for at least another long, grueling twenty minutes. Every so often, one of the guys would yell out, "You okay, how you doing?"

"Just a walk in the park," I'd answer. I kept jabbing myself with the catch pole, which was really annoying, and before long, I realized I had left it behind me; I could feel it with my foot. Just what I wanted to do was scoot backward and get the darn thing, but then I needed it; I didn't want to meet our buddy, the lion, without it. I knew that in this cramped space, I could fend him off with it if I needed to. So not only was it my way to hopefully catch the lion, it was also a form of protection, though a pretty poor one. I mean, c'mon, what's some metal rod with a noose on the end going to do against an angry lion? Probably make him madder, don't you think? But it was all I had, and somehow, in my heart, I never felt it would be a problem. So I wasn't concerned.

I'd go a foot, or so, then shine the light down the dark passage looking for blond lion fur or shining eyes looking back at me; nothing so far.

I was starting to get the pushing with my toes pulling with my hands' motion down so well while holding the noose in one hand and the flashlight in the other that I went about eight more feet without thinking of shining the light ahead of me.

Holding the light up, I turn it forward so I can see and *aarrrg-ghhhh!* His face is just three feet from mine. I violently throw my head back, reacting to get away. *Bam!* I pound it against the floor, inches above me. *Ouch,* in shock and pain, I instinctively throw my head down and plant my face in the dirt. Ouch again! *Bam!* I pound it into the floor above me again, and again its face plant in the dirt.

Bam, head, face plant; *bam,* head, face plant. I felt like a cartoon.

Finally getting ahold of myself, I brace for a confrontation and shine the light again towards the face I just saw, all the while hoping it would scare him to run. But there it was again. Almost another *bam* and face plant, but I controlled myself better this time.

Humm…his eyes are closed, and he's not moving. So I poke him strongly with the catch pole. What! He's dead!

"Hey, I found him!" I yell out.

"You did? Can you get him? What's he doing?"

"It looks like he's eating what's left of a human hand," I tease. After a short, deep silence, I hear frantic movements and running around bumping into things sounds. Then a long few moments later, I hear the calm, collected voice of my longtime friend Brian. "Greg, you should see the panic you just caused. I don't know if they'll ever recover. But I know you're teasing. What did you really find?"

Getting the noose around his neck after about the fifth try, I tug, and his whole body moves forward. Looking at him after all the buildup to this moment, I find it hard to believe he's dead. I look intently into the face one more time just to make sure. I don't want any more surprises. Yep, he's still dead, good.

Backing back down the passageway seemed much faster, except as I'd move down, I'd pull Leo, the dead lion, up too far, and he'd bump into my head. Gross! After the third time, I figured I'd better change something up, or I'd have stinky dead lion smell all over my hat. All I had to do was loosen my hold on the noose pole down a bit, and the extra two feet made the difference.

Finally reaching the opening to the hole, I'm so relieved to be done. I jump scoot joyfully out, "Yeaaa," and then, seemingly out of nowhere, the head comes rolling and bouncing down the mound of dirt past my feet towards the men behind me. "What?" I yell out. "How'd that happen?" To see grown men jumping and dancing so gingerly and convoluting their bodies in such funny ways to keep away from the rolling lion's head was hilarious. It stopped, so they stopped, and we all broke out laughing. What a cartoon scene that was.

Looking back in the black hole, I figure that somewhere along the way, the head came off of the body, and I never noticed. Nuts! Just what I wanted was to go back in there again and retrieve more dead rotten lion parts. I had to go farther back than I expected, and sure enough, there was the headless body lying there.

Putting the noose around a leg, I pull, and it simply pops off the body. Oh, great, this thing is so rotten it's falling apart; I'm not carrying this carcass out piece by piece, no way. Finally, I strategically get the other leg and pull very carefully, and it comes along fine, but only if I pull slow and easy. Backing out again ever so carefully, I reach the mouth of the hole again, but this time with the rest of the body.

Everyone was so happy that they weren't the ones to have to do the great rescue that they spent extra time congratulating me on the fine job. You find out what people are made of from the most unexpected things.

"Man, that was intense; I could hardly stand the suspense!" the fireman exclaimed.

"I could never have done that," the homeowner piped in, shaking his head as he spoke.

"I wouldn't have even tried," the ranger admitted very dryly with a half-smile. I liked the ranger; he was a very matter-of-fact kind of man, no pretense, no games, and a sense of humor. I let the audience gather the head and the carcass and put it in a plastic trash bag. They insisted, and I wasn't going to argue. At least the ranger was willing to dispose of all the stinking body parts.

"Here you go, Greg, $40; no, wait a minute; that's too much. I need some of that; give me $20 back. There, $20 for your trouble."

"You're so generous, Brian."

"I know, I only charged him $100; I should have charged him ten times that, but I made the decision over the phone without seeing the real situation, and I have to keep my word," Brian exclaimed.

I had prayed in the Spirit for a long time while I walked around our neighborhood the night before. I usually wait for nightfall, then head out; it's more private that way. The Lord shows me all kinds of things, and it also prepares the next day and beyond for me. I like getting up in the morning knowing the day has already been prepared for me and all I have to do is walk it out. Other folks pray in the morning for their day, but I pray the night before; it just works out best for me that way.

Anyway, if the Lord doesn't tell me straight out what to do, I go by the peace I feel in my heart and then my mind. I had peace the whole time in this situation (except the little claustrophobic episode in the hole); there was no caution, no red flags, no fear. So I knew that going after the mountain lion the way I did was not a problem; otherwise, there would have been a warning for me, and there wasn't. Many folks approach a situation like this with fear first. I don't. I start with what is happening, what isn't happening, and what I can do about it. In this instance, it was caution and respect for what a cornered wild animal can do. It determines everything about what can and cannot or should not be done. But fear creates a filter where perception and truth are altered, twisted. None of us can afford to make decisions from an altered perception or a truth that has been twisted. Life stinks (like a dead lion) when we make that mistake.

Second Corinthians 10:4-5 says, "For the weapons of our warfare are not of the flesh, but divinely powerful for the destruction of fortresses. We are destroying speculations and every lofty thing raised up against the knowledge of God, and we are taking every thought captive to the obedience of Christ."

Fear can become such a fortress in our minds that we can't overcome it. But if we start making an effort to take those thoughts captive, to control them by replacing them with what is true, then we have changed our belief about something, which changes how we act, what we say and what we do.

It's pretty powerful; those two scriptures are simple yet profound and have changed my life. My decision to say no to fear and speak to my mind changed everything for me, and I was able to continue. If I hadn't have done that, I know I wouldn't have made it. What we choose to believe is so mighty; it's life-changing, either for good or for bad.

I didn't need to stop and pray through this situation when we came upon it, I had already prayed the night before, and I knew the Lord had prepared my way. I knew what to do; then, I simply followed what I could see and whatever I heard the Holy Spirit say down in my heart. I make the plan He directs the path proverbs says, and again, in the psalms, it says they shall be led forth with peace. Sometimes things are a whole lot more simple than we try to make them.

Witch Doctor in Guatemala

Renee called very bothered for her people in Guatemala; it was an orphanage and school in a Mayan community that she oversaw. The local witch doctor had put all the names of the people in her project on a death list and was actively working to kill them with his witchcraft. Some of the teachers had already had some bad things happen to them. Part of a rafter fell out of the ceiling and smacked one of them on the head. Another cut her knee badly, and it quickly got painfully infected and abscessed. A third got weirdly sick. Another couldn't even teach because she was so tormented by fear she just stood and shook. Dread blanketed the whole village. It felt like death was winning.

Rats had infested the Christian part of the project; they had never been overrun by rats and all their filth before. It was disgusting. The fear and dread over the place were so thick everyone could feel it. Some of the children just sat and cried.

So, Renee set up a Skype call between her, the teachers, and Michelle, and me. Renee could see them, but we had no visual on our screen though we could hear them perfectly. When

I asked the Lord what to do as I prepared for this time, I was shown to simply pray as He led and teach them how to speak the Scriptures with their names in it. First thing after the session started, I bound Satan in Jesus' name and sealed them and the situation with the blood of Jesus so they would be safe and there would be no spiritual interference.

Everything had to be translated, so I had to speak in short snippets. First into Spanish and then into Mayan. I told them if they felt any discomfort, any pain, or sudden sickness, anything out of the ordinary during this Skype session to let me know so I could stop and take care of it. They had a few pains and problems trying to bother them at first, but when I prayed as they occurred, they all went away. It was witchcraft trying to interfere. They were seeing from the start that God would answer their prayers. That He is greater than the witchcraft, they hadn't experienced anything like that before with God.

There were a number of things I wanted to teach but waiting for things to be translated and our time restriction caused me to change my whole plan and just focus on whatever was going to be short and the most effective for them. Here was a group of people that had been cursed and was in danger of more torment, being hurt, or even dying. So my answer had to speak directly to their situation, and it had to work for them, and it had to work right now, or it was worthless. It didn't matter what I couldn't do; it only mattered about what God can do, regardless of my flaws and time constraints.

I took Psalm 91 and showed them how to pray and put themselves or someone else in it. I Explained how each part of the scripture applied to them as a group and personally. All based on their lives and specific circumstances, to make it applicable for them. I also read some other scriptures specifically against witchcraft for them so they could learn how to do the same for themselves. As I read the Scriptures, I put each of their names in it so they could hear and understand what to do, then turn around and do the same themselves. It's all in the power of the Word we speak, and I showed them how to use it to deliver them from the curses and the torment.

They all had seen the power of witchcraft before and were afraid of what might happen to them. It was common for terrible things, even tormented deaths, to happen to people who had been cursed, so they were greatly afraid for themselves and their families. They didn't know that God loved them and had the power to not only deliver them but destroy the witchcraft and set them all free. Not just today but forever. How sad that their version of Christianity didn't have God's power in it, though they had heard about it and now desperately needed it.

They were nervous about directly confronting the witch doctor with the Scriptures as we were doing (even though it was not face to face but from a distance); they were afraid of a retaliation of curses coming upon them, and things were already so bad that the whole project was falling apart with despair and demonic accidents. But they had hope. Nothing they had done so far helped at all, and they were willing to at least try. Besides, their director told them there was someone who could help them, and they wanted to see if it was true. Either the Bible is true, and we have power over evil, or we don't. Pretty simple.

First off, peace fell upon our group. It was a great peace, almost like you could touch it. They hadn't had peace for days,

71

and I didn't even pray for it. The Holy Spirit just moved, and mightily at that. Then it fell upon the whole project, a peace that everyone could actually feel. That alone spoke loudly to them all that this Christian God is bigger than they thought.

Then a short time into the session, demons began manifesting in one of the Mayan teachers. I couldn't see her, but they said she was contorting weirdly and making animal noises and other things. I waited a long moment then bound the demons in the name of Jesus.

"Now, what is she doing?" I asked.

"The demons have stopped, and she seems to be in her right mind," they responded. The Lord had specifically shown me not to cast anything out of her now but that He would deliver her in time.

That demonstration of God's power over the demons was both astonishing and refreshing to them. They needed to see it so they could believe in His power and move forward. Otherwise, all was lost. They needed to see evidence of the demons first to know they were there; then, they needed the demonstration that the name of Jesus is all-powerful and that the words from the Bible that we speak actually work.

They also needed to know which one of their own was actually sabotaging them and working with the witch doctor against them. Now there is no doubt. The demons in her proved it to everyone, and because of that unexpected incident, she confessed because the power of God so convicted her, and she was humiliated in front of the others and because her dark secret had been revealed. All of which the Lord used to show her and the others that greater is He who is in us than he who is in the world, or the witch doctor. Now they all wanted to know more about the Lord.

God is good!

After that half hour with the Christian teachers, the whole community changed and got brighter, they said. They described it as like a dark, almost transparent fog had lifted. The peace stayed mightily with them, and fear was no longer controlling them. The witchcraft had been destroyed. They began to pray differently and decree the Word over their lives, some not much, some more than others. One teacher began taking time every day with her classes and teaching them what she had learned. Those little Mayan kids are now speaking and praying the Word over their families. It has impacted the whole village and changed all their lives. Children trained in the way they should go are a treasure without measure.

Isn't it amazing that a half-hour skyping with people in another part of the world actually changed a whole community and destroyed the hold that witchcraft had on them for generations?

The power in the name of Jesus and the power in the Scriptures spoken out is truly wonderful and amazing.

Swarmed by Bees

A man we'd never met before came to us for prayer and got swarmed by bees and stung.

We had walked up the path to the meadow so I could show him some things and tell him what the Lord had shown me specifically for him. I had a few analogies with short explanations to share. The Lord wanted to show him some things that he could relate to that would help him understand and also confirm a number of personal issues for him. He was at a desperate place in his life and needed some help outside of his trusted circle. He's a man of authority with big responsibilities in nations around the world. So for him, this was no small encounter. He wanted help; he needed answers. The fresh mountain air, the amazing view, all the flowers, and the beautiful path to get up there are always inspiring. Even for us, and we've been up to it hundreds of times. I knew that there were things the Lord would show him during this walk, and it was important for him to get as much as possible during our short time together.

They were yellow jackets, and they seemingly came out of nowhere. It was amazing, one moment, we were walking along, talking, and the next, in the blink of an eye, he was being swarmed and couldn't get away. I knew as it was happening that it was curse-related.

The Lord then showed me (it was like a vision, I actually saw it like a translucent picture that I could see through, superimposed over the situation) that he was dragging the curses with him. It was odd as I had never seen it like that before. That the curses someone is dragging could bring a natural destruction upon them, and it was happening before my eyes. Somewhere there was fear, and it was drawing it out. I knew it from experience, but I had never actually seen it, not at least like this.

I saw that he had a belt like a thick leather belt around his waist, and trailing behind him from the leather belt were these leather-like ropes with large black crystals tied to the ends of them. As I looked, I was immediately shown that all of these were the curses. Many came from other nations. And every curse he had made agreements with was affecting his life and bringing problems and even destructions down upon his head. Wow, interesting.

He went into survival mode and started to panic. He didn't know what else to do but stand and fight and try to protect himself, thrashing his arms wildly in the air. Can't blame him; it was intense. Pain and dying were all he could think of. He was very allergic to bee stings and would die within minutes after being stung without immediate intervention. Michelle was closest to him and saw the problem and took charge commanding him loudly about what to do. He wasn't thinking clearly at the moment; he was just reacting to the chaos, the pain, and the fear. In the panic of the moment, he couldn't hear her if she didn't yell. She ran to him, got behind him, and said, "Move!

Move down the path! Quickly! Don't wait, go now! go now!" she cried out.

All the while, as he is swatting at the angry yellow jackets, they were landing on him, violently stinging everywhere on his bare skin and even through his clothes. I could see the swarm madly swirling around him. It was surreal. It was not a pretty sight. One landed on the front of Michelle's blouse, and she promptly smacked him down; it was the only one that got near to her. The rest stayed away even though she was standing with John in the midst of the swarm. At that moment, she had no fear, no thought of *what if they attack me?* Her whole attention was focused on rescuing John. As I watched, the moments seemed to drag on in slow motion forever, but really the whole thing only lasted a few seconds. God's protection for her was amazing; she never got stung once.

Now fear had completely taken over his mind, and he wasn't sure what to do. I understand why.

The stings cause his throat to swell, and he can't breathe or swallow.

It all happens in mere seconds. And then you die.

And here we are on the side of a mountain miles from medical help, and it was beginning to rain. Things couldn't have become more miserable.

After getting him farther down the mountain safely away from the swarm, Michelle laid her hands on his back and began rebuking Satan and standing against this attack in Jesus' name. Michelle asked if he was okay, and he said, "Yes, I will be okay."

That decision to trust God and to speak it laid the groundwork for his survival. It established his determination to live.

Otherwise, he might be dead.

It's amazing how sometimes seemingly simple things make the difference for us between life or death, and usually, it's just a decision, a simple decision, and a few words that we speak.

He gingerly took a few steps towards me, wanting more help, so I looked him in the eyes and repeated the question. "Are you okay?"

He said again, strongly, "Yes, I will be okay!"

I knew the gravity of the situation and needed him to speak it again.

I needed to see in his eyes where he really stood.

I needed to hear his heart.

Because it is written, and it is so true that "life and death are in the power of the tongue" (Proverbs 18:21), and again, "As a man thinks in his heart so is he" (Proverbs 23:7, NKJV).

Once I saw his stand in faith to live and not die, it gave me hope.

His determination to survive suddenly had become very strong. He had chosen life. I could now stand strongly with him.

I prayed while laying my hands on him, standing on the steps of the path in the gently falling rain:

"Death to the poison, life to John, life to his flesh in Jesus' name."

"Death to the poison, life to John, life to his flesh in Jesus' name."

"Death to the poison, life to John, life to his flesh in Jesus' name."

Then I turned, starting back down the path, and said, "Let's get back to the house." I was anxious to get him out of the woods, the place of pain and the wet, and into the comfort of our home where he could relax. We needed to sort through some things. Because I didn't see any immediate results, I wanted to give the prayers some time to work, let the Lord move in his mind and his body.

Michelle followed along behind him as we made our way down, speaking healing scriptures strongly over him and praying in the Spirit. The soft mountain rain began to fall harder, the fresh water streaming down our faces, cooling the summer day and seemingly rinsing the pain and dirt of this nasty situation away for all of us.

Before I prayed, his right arm and hand were already starting to swell, and it had only been a little more than a minute. Think of it. In only seconds his body had begun swelling everywhere he had been stung; all his visible parts were already noticeably distorted and larger.

By the time we got back to the house and sat down, the swelling had already disappeared, and all was looking well. We marveled at how quickly the Lord had worked. It was probably a little less than five minutes. The power of prayer is amazing. The power of what we choose to believe is also amazing.

John *believed* he could be delivered from death, he strongly chose life, and he lived.

The Father wonderfully and miraculously healed him, and when we prayed, He also removed the curses I had seen and their roots. John was delivered from many things that day, not just the poison from the stings. He had hoped to meet God and experience a miracle, which is exactly what happened. Though it definitely wasn't like any of us expected. Watching God work like that sure helps to renew your faith that He heals and is Almighty and will help us out no matter how desperate the circumstances are. "Just believe" took on a whole new fresh meaning for all of us that day. John is alive today because of a miracle. Instead of "dead man walking," we had "live man happy"!

Quite a start to a relationship, don't you think?

Enjoy Life

Take a moment to enjoy the good and
simple things in life.
One thing that has helped us immensely.
And made life so much better,
especially during hardship,
is to make ourselves take time for each other,
for friends and for loved ones.
Like it says in Thessalonians,
God gives us all good things to enjoy.
When we made ourselves take that time,
we found that life was much better, fuller,
somehow it gave us hope
during the hopeless times.
Joy during the depressing times.
Life during times of dread.
We were rich even when we had nothing.
We now practice it no matter what is going on.
So take the time and enjoy
the good and simple things in life.

The Cave

According to my cousin Ronnie, people had been going through this cave for years. It was part of an old sinkhole on the ranch that, when the ground had fallen in, it revealed the mouths of these caves that were already there. It was pretty big, at least fifty yards across. Ronnie is about fifteen years older than me, and he and his friends had explored it many times as young boys. The directions were simple, and the description intriguing. "You take the tunnel until you end up in a small room. You find the opening from there and go through it up into the music room. So named because when you hit the different boulders, they each have a distinct and unique sound." Well, that sounded fun, and we're always up for an adventure.

So off we go Michelle and me, our three sons about thirteen, twelve, and ten, and Don Garrett, Ronnie's grandson, who was our boy's age. "Oh ya," Ronnie adds as we enter the mouth of the cave, "keep an eye out for snakes; sometimes, you'll find rattlers back in there." Michelle cringed when she heard that. And the boys? Their attitude was, snakes? Who cares about snakes; this is going to be fun. And off we went, them running, us walking with Michelle's motherly admonitions about being careful and watch out for snakes echoing off the walls into the blackness of the cave behind them.

We had three flashlights between the six of us, so before we started on our adventure, I had every other one of us carry one, so we could spread the light out as much as possible. The four boys were so excited to go exploring that it was hard to hold them back, but I made them wait for us. There was a chance we'd run into an animal or a rattlesnake or who knows what. It was just wiser to stay together to start out with. It helped a lot to know where we were going and that there weren't any other passageways to get lost in. Ronnie figured it was about fifty to seventy-five yards back to the music room. Sounded doable to me.

The first twenty yards were great, we could walk standing up, and the light from the outside was still reflecting down the white limestone corridor. Then the roof of the cave started to slope down, and we had to start bending our heads to fit. Soon it's about three feet tall, and we had to crawl or duck walk for about another twenty yards. Great if you're in shape, painful if you're not.

As we went along, there were a few other areas like little sub-caves and cubby holes off the main tunnel; some were like a closet, others went about ten feet back. Most were filled with the debris of old dens and the bones of dead animals that had been killed and dragged into the cave and eaten: rabbits, sheep, deer, birds, snakes, and whatever. It added a dimension of dread to the whole experience if such a thing scared you. So, what ate them? Mostly coyotes and foxes. Also, there were piles of guano here and there though we didn't see any bats.

Seeing the bones of the animals that had been eaten did not sit well with Michelle. No way. Her mother made her watch scary movies even when she didn't want to when she was young, and they played havoc with her imagination to this day. To make it worse, her mother would say, "Don't cover your eyes; this is the best part," and take her hands down, so she had to watch. She was having a really hard time, all because of those stupid movies. She was struggling to get past her vain imagination of vicious things springing out to kill us.

All she could think about was animals screaming out of the dark to attack us or some strange, angry, man-eating creature and not being able to get away. Once she saw that nothing was there and realized she wasn't going to be eaten, she settled down. That is until she started thinking about snakes slithering around. Training the light very carefully everywhere in a couple of lairs off to the side so she could see there weren't any snakes or menacing eyes looking back at us took a while, but she was finally okay, and we were able to move on. (A number of years later, the Lord showed her what she needed to know and set her free from this fear junk. What amazing freedom she has now!) Today, though, it was a real battle for her.

The boys could care less about the bones or snakes; they just found them interesting and had moved on farther into the cave. (We didn't allow scary movies or scary stories to create vain imaginations when they were young, so they had no fear.) I could hear their excited chatter as they made their way, but now they were far enough ahead that we couldn't see even a hint of light. I called out to them, hoping they would hear me so they would stop and wait for us. I didn't want us all to get separated, and Michelle felt much more comfortable having them nearby. She needed to know they were safe and hadn't been eaten by anything. Once fear starts to take over, it interferes with everything, and it's really annoying when you're not afraid, and someone else's fear interferes with what you're doing. Thank God Michelle's fear didn't get on anybody else. We were all having quite the interesting experience.

Garrett came back to meet us after a while and took us to where the others were waiting. We had now moved from some light to no light. The "black as ink can't see your hand in front of your face" kind of dark. We could only hear things or feel them; that's all. Also, the roof of the cave was now low enough that we had to crawl on our hands and knees. That wouldn't have been so bad except that the floor of the cave wasn't dirt; it was sharp chips of rock, and we were wearing shorts, so it was murder on our knees. The boys, of course, didn't even notice. When you are young and on an adventure, sometimes nothing bothers you.

We reached a place where Garrett says we have to squirm through. The guys on the other side shined their lights so we could see, but the passage was pretty tight. They said that was the only difficult spot and that we'd make it through fine. We trusted each other; we all knew what we could and could not do.

The hole looked to be about 18 x 24, doable but tight-almost an intimidating kind of tight. The kids went right through on their stomachs. There was no way I could make it on my stomach. The angle of the stones made it feel like I would break my back going at it like that. So I backed out and rolled over on my back and pushed myself through. It took some work, but I was able to get my head and shoulders through to the other side. Laying there facing up, I shined my flashlight up to see what was there. A large crack was going up about thirty feet where long ago large rocks had fallen and wedged themselves together above our heads. You could tell that if one of them was moved, they would all fall on top of us, and it all came to a point at the tight squeeze. I pondered just how safe this really was and realized this had probably happened way back when the sinkhole was created. Nothing was going to fall on us. Satisfied all was well, I pulled myself through the tight squeeze and sat on the other side, shining my light so Michelle could see how to go. Coaching her through, she now wanted to see what was up above us that I had been looking at. Shining the light up the large crack, she saw the rocks and almost started to hyperventilate; it scared her so bad. All she could think about was how they were going to fall on us and kill us and block the cave. Panic was trying to push itself in. The vain imaginations of all the bad things that could possibly happen were pouring through her mind, and she couldn't stop them.

She wasn't going one more inch! "Get me out of here." She started going back and didn't care if it was with a light or without a light, with me or without me; it just didn't matter. I couldn't let her go all that way back by herself in a pitch-black cave groping along until she made it back to the entrance tormented and driven by fear. And I really didn't want to go all the way back to the pickup. It was a long way back out. I tried to convince her all was well, no one was going to die, but she wasn't having it. She was in great distress. So I pulled myself painfully and reluctantly back through the tight squeeze, and we started what was for me a long, miserable trek back out.

Once we reached the place where you could barely see because there was a slight light, she sped up and was gone. I mean, that girl was gone! Leaving me in her dust, she didn't care; she just wanted out!

Our cousins were there waiting patiently, relaxing on the tailgate of the pickup, peacefully enjoying the pleasant afternoon. Beverly says, "Wow, where'd you come from? You didn't come out the same way you went in."

"Yes, we did."

"No, you didn't."

Now both women were in a real tizzy. How could that happen when there's only one cave? Looking around to solve the mystery, it turns out there are two mouths to the same cave, not two caves. They each went back about twenty feet before joining the main tunnel, and we didn't even notice that until we came out. Interesting!

Seeing that Michelle was now okay and totally relieved, I went back to catch up with the kids inside. Going on my knees over the sharp rocks again was almost unbearable because the pain was so great. So I focused on where I was going and not the pain, or I wouldn't have made it, all the while keeping my knees up as much as possible. I spoke out, "I can do all things through Christ who strengthens me," over and over. It helped ease my mind. Going in the first time, it wasn't painful, just uncomfortable. I was amazed at how that had changed this time. Troubled circumstances definitely can change our perceptions.

Through the tight squeeze again and now down the passageway. Nobody was waiting for me this time; they had moved on. It got smaller and smaller within about ten feet and tight enough that I had to pull myself through on my stomach. Then it came to a ninety-degree turn. Now that was challenging. At that point, I could feel Michelle's fear trying to come upon me. It felt like it had been following me. I was looking at how constrained I was and how difficult the situation looked, and I began to be afraid. I could feel panic was trying to come into me, into my mind, so I cried out loudly, "No! No, I rebuke you in the name of Jesus, I don't accept you!" and I could actually feel it lift off. I was so relieved! I felt peace envelop me and immediately started to breathe better, and my body loosened up, and I could move easily again. Fear can really mess you up. I had to work hard to control my thoughts this time, to keep fear out, to keep it from becoming like a stronghold in my mind. The words I was speaking helped keep that from happening. It kept my mind free.

> For though we walk in the flesh, we do not war according to the flesh, for the weapons of our warfare are not of the flesh, but divinely powerful for the destruction of fortresses. We are destroying speculations and every lofty thing raised up against the knowledge of God, and we are taking every thought captive to the obedience of Christ.
>
> 2 Corinthians 10:3-5

"For God has not given us a spirit of fear, but of power and of love and of a sound mind" (2 Timothy 1:7, NKJV).

I was quite relieved that Michelle wasn't with me because I knew there was no way she'd make it through this part. As a matter of fact, I wouldn't have continued from there if I hadn't known the end wasn't far away. It was very difficult crawling through. It was like crawling on your stomach and forcing yourself through a culvert that was just big enough to barely fit in.

The tunnel finally opened up a bit which allowed me to move and breathe easier. Then all of a sudden, there I was, almost falling headfirst into a room I could actually stand up in; it was about 10 x 10 with a high ceiling. Boy, was that a relief from fighting to fit through the tunnel. Looking around, I saw the faint glow of a light on one of the rocks and went over and found the short tunnel that was the entrance to the next room: the music room. It, too, had a high stone ceiling, coming to a rounded point overhead that made it look like the inside of a European cathedral.

The boys were jumping around from boulder to boulder and hitting the big rocks with the smaller rocks in their hands. "Listen, Dad." They excitedly pounded out some drum music for me on the various boulders, and it sounded great. Their enthusiasm was contagious. The variety of different sounds you could make on all the different rocks was astounding. No wonder Ronnie liked it when he was young. I found a couple of rocks and joined in. We were playing a caveman concert with a stone drum symphony. The light from our flashlights placed strategically around the room was highlighting our faces and casting amazing shadows that danced across the rocks and disappeared into black as we played. It was surreal. For a while, time seemed to stand still. It felt like we were on a musical bridge with our ancient ancestors touching the past and the present at the same time. How fascinating.

We enjoyed playing rhythms and making noise for a long time; then, I noticed the air was starting to get stale—time to go. Since I was so much slower than they were, I let them go ahead of me and told them they didn't have to wait for me to keep up. They crawled quickly through all the tight spots then scurried out. Garrett went with them then came back to check on me because I was taking so long. I was fine. Just not as quick as four small athletic boys in a hurry to get out, so it took me a lot longer.

Exiting that cave into the sunshine was like coming from death back to life, especially after crawling across those sharp rocks again. It was truly exhilarating to see life, to feel life; I couldn't get enough of the sunshine. I closed my eyes with my face to the warm afternoon sun and could actually feel it filling my body with life.

What an experience! I still get bits and pieces of revelation about things every time I think about it, and it's been years since we did that.

Also, I have found that the greater my revelation of God's love for us, the less fear I have to contend with.

"There is no fear in love; but perfect love casts out fear, because fear involves punishment, and the one who fears is not perfected in love" (1 John 4:18).

I meditate on this regularly and pray for more revelation because it makes a huge difference in the way I think and believe about things. The more I know God loves me, the easier things are when I have to pray and believe for the answer or the miracle.

Michelle's Broken Ankle

The move was brutal. We had been working nonstop for almost twenty-four hours, just Michelle and I. No help this time. Everyone had other engagements or just didn't want to help. I can't blame them. Helping someone move is a big commitment and a lot of work. And this particular move was definitely both. It was a long, arduous drive through the mountains, over Berthoud Pass, and down into Golden. Two hours one way by car, somewhere close to three hours in a truck full of furniture and possessions. The truck was free; that's why we were using it, but it only held about two rooms worth of stuff at a time, and we were moving from a three-bedroom home with a full basement and a garage to a small two-bedroom townhouse with no garage. Because of some urgent matters, we didn't have time to sort through our things in the mountains, so we were just going to stack the boxes in the new place and sort through them over the next week or so.

Some friends were watching the boys, which helped a lot. They were just big enough to be in the way as the oldest was two years old, and the other was one; the third one hadn't been born yet.

Backing up to the front door, we looked at each other and smiled; we were almost done. It was 2 a.m. in the morning, and this load was it, and we were tired, really tired. Unloading this wouldn't take long, and we'd be back on the road home so we could sleep a few hours, then pick up the kids and finish. This arduous task would be done. Relief was just around the corner.

Jumping down from the back of the truck, I could hear Michelle's ankle snap loudly as she landed on the ground. The sound brought instant pain back to my mind as I remembered when I had broken my ankles. Her face was filled with agony as she felt the excruciating pain surge through her body. She began writhing on the ground letting out the deep groans that only happen with such great pain and distress; her face was already white with shock. All of a sudden, without even thinking, I shouted intensely, "Ankle be healed in the name of Jesus." Then this powerful knowing of "it's done!" came over me, and I just knew she had been healed. "Get up," I commanded, "and walk!" (You might think Michelle was offended by this command, but she wasn't because she knew I was speaking in faith and that I loved her and cared about her.) Again, the words came out without me even thinking about it. The only way I can explain it is that I had this knowing that wasn't in my mind; it was in my heart, we had an emergency, and I had to do something to help her, so I spoke what came out first. Amazingly that simple prayer had worked, and Michelle was okay. Actually, it's all in the power of the name of Jesus, and I had in this instant, special revelation of that this time. The Holy Spirit gave it to me; I didn't wonder or even question; I just knew it.

Reaching out from the bed of the truck to help her up, she gave me her hand, and, pushing up with her good leg, she lifted her wounded foot. The pain wasn't just in her ankle but was throbbing throughout her whole foot and up her leg. She said the pain then moved as if it was pulled out of the back of her ankle, and then it was gone. It was just gone. Stepping over and over again on that foot to test it, she could hardly believe it was healed, and amazingly that it was healed in an instant. Then she did a happy dance.

This was one of those *wow* experiences that you only hear about, and we just had it ourselves. When you have one of these, it totally changes your belief system. It was almost a three-hour drive back up into the mountains, and about every five minutes, one of us would marvel again at the miracle that happened. We'd never had anything happen instantly like that before; it was truly astonishing and wonderful. Now we had no doubt that God could and would actually do such a thing for us; we lived it, Michelle felt it, we saw it with our own eyes. The power in the name of Jesus really works. Our prayer life has never been the same.

Michelle's Dream

For a number of years, Michelle often had a recurring dream about a beautiful home. She would walk into the living room, and everything was in perfect order and beautiful down to the smallest detail. As she walked into the other rooms of this house, they were still nice but got progressively worse, first a little messy, then a lot messier and dirty, and then into the kitchen, which was a disgusting disaster.

Interestingly there was a door that was like an entrance door that opened suddenly into the kitchen, and then the exit door from the kitchen was on the other side of the room. Looking around, she noticed the ceiling was ruined, hanging in pieces reaching all the way down to the counter, old dirty dishes were pilled high, water was drip, drip, dripping from the leaky faucet, dust, mold, and filth were everywhere.

This time in the dream sitting at the table by the exit door was what looked like a person dressed in white; the hair was long and a grungy white and very stringy and waxy. This being was facing the opposite doorway. When she walked up to it, the head turned around and looked at her, but the body remained facing the other direction. She knew it was the same demon as in all the past dreams trying to intimidate her again, though it was never found in the kitchen before it was usually going up a stairway and was always very scary, but this time, Michelle had no fear, and she said to it, "Get out and don't come back."

When the demon stood up, it was big, more than twice as tall as she was. It started to run through the house, going upstairs and walkways to new and higher levels like before. She was chasing it for what seemed a long time and then felt that she should stop because they were going somewhere and yet nowhere at the same time. Something was wrong. Somehow, she knew he was leading her to a place she couldn't return from if he could just get her to follow. He would run ahead and then stop to wait for her to catch up. This happened every time she had this dream, and every time she would come to that place that felt dangerous and life-threatening, she would stop, and great fear would come over her, and then the dream would end, and she would wake up feeling abused and tormented.

But this time, as he was leading her on and on, they entered a realm more dangerous than any of the others, something beyond where she had ever been before, which when she realized it, she stopped herself and commanded him to stop. She yelled, "Get on your knees and say Jesus is Lord."

He bowed his head and said quietly, "Jesus is Lord."

She said, "Say it again, say it louder." He kept his head bowed and did exactly as she said. She didn't think about what she was saying; it just came up out of her with incredible power. Even on his knees, he was so big that his head was higher than hers. Then she angrily commanded the demon to leave and never return in Jesus' name. It got up and ran through a revolving glass door. As the demon ran out, it turned right around and ran swiftly back to the door, trying to come back in.

He smacked full force into the glass, but it did not open; it didn't even move but stood strong against the power of the impact. When the demon hit the glass door in her dream, it also hit so hard against my back that it woke me up from a sound sleep. It actually moved me across the bed so that my back bumped into Michelle's back. I groggily turned to Michelle, very puzzled, and asked, "What the heck is going on?" I thought she had been kicking me in the back, and I couldn't figure out why. She told me what she had just dreamt, and all I remember is saying "oh" because now I understood and then rolled over and went back to sleep. I know, I know, wonderful encouragement for her in a great time of need. Oh well, I made up for it in the morning once I was awake, clear-headed, and thinking straight.

Lying in bed and pondering what had just happened, it was like a light of knowledge suddenly came on in Michelle's head, flooding her mind with understanding about the demon, the dream, and all the things that had happened in it. She had asked the Lord for an interpretation. He was answering her prayer. She realized then that this dream kept happening because she didn't know the real authority that she had in Jesus's name or how to use it. When she used His name with the authority He gave her, it stopped this recurring, tormenting nightmare and got rid of the demon associated with it. What's amazing is how simple and yet powerful the answer was.

As she continued in deep thought, she saw that the house represented her. The outside was well kept and clean, but the inside got progressively messier because there were areas in her life that were in good shape and others that needed to be renewed and cleaned, even remodeled. She found out she could take authority over those things and the dirt of iniquity that up until now had been hidden and get rid of it all. She asked the Lord to show her what needed to be cleaned with the blood of Jesus and how to do it. That's the important part, how to do it. And the Holy Spirit showed exactly what to do. It began a great journey that set her free from generational things, fear, and failure. This dream never occurred again. Yea!

She was certainly amazed that there was anything like this in place in her life. She had been a Christian for quite a while and had repented much, and the Lord had freed her from many things. So how could all those other areas still be there? She learned that our Christian walk is actually a journey. And because the Lord will continually work on the issues of our lives, I suppose you could call us a work in progress until we get to heaven. Because only then and there will we be perfected, no problems, no blemishes, no faults, no sin, no temptation.

Now she is free from that long-running and tormenting nightmare and from the things that held it in place. She asked the Lord, "What happened when that demon tried to get back into our house and couldn't?" She felt Him speak into her heart that her husband was a covering for her, and then Jesus is a covering for us both and our family. How great and comforting it was for her to see Jesus and her husband as her covering. A double covering that neither of us knew existed. Heck, I never thought that because of our marriage covenant that somehow, I'd become a covering, not only for her but our children also.

How amazing that when it hit the glass door, the demon was actually running into me, her husband, and the truth that protects me. The evil couldn't hurt me or get through me back to her because, as her husband, I'm a covering for her. That anointing is the Lord's, and it is upon me; I didn't know it was there until now. Even when I'm asleep, and I don't know what's going on, it's working. And then the Lord is the covering for us all.

"For the husband is the head of the wife as Christ also is the head of the church. He himself being the Savior of the body" (Ephesians 5:23).

There was also more interpretation to the dream that had to do with Michelle personally and what else she needed to do to get cleaned up and healed, which she did, and it changed her life. She helped me, and now she helps others so the Lord can heal them too.

But that is another story.

Repair the Ruins

May the ruins in your heart be restored;
the foundation of truth be made strong.
May the roof be repaired that covers your head
and your memories cleansed and made long.
May the path to your mind be a beautiful garden
growing flowers of love and of joy and of light.
May the door to your heart be secured with discretion.
That your hope day by day may be bright.
May you rise up now healed, in a strength not your own
take His mantle; it will carry you through.
Every good, every bad, every happy, every sad.
May you live well whatever you do.

Lost at Havasupai Falls

Looking down, he saw that both shoes had become untied. Garrett was at the bottom of the Grand Canyon at a place between Havasupai Falls and Beaver Falls on the Indian reservation. They had just finished playing in the large pool of water beneath the falls and had decided to go exploring. Kneeling on one knee in the red dirt, he looked up at his friends and said, "Hey, wait a minute, I've got to tie my shoes." Quickly taking care of business, he stood up and looked around. No friends. How could they have disappeared so quickly? Why didn't they wait? Which way did they go? How did he not hear them leave? This is sure odd.

They had stopped at a fork in the path. Choosing the way they were all supposed to be headed, he went a short distance expecting to catch up but couldn't find them, so he stopped and looked carefully in all directions; at the same time, he was listening for any sound that would tell him where they went. Starting to feel uneasy, he had this thought, why not ask the Lord what to do? When he did, he heard this answer down inside, "To keep on going," so he did, continually looking for any sign of his friends.

Up the path, he noticed a set of ancient-looking ladders leaning against a small cliff. Drawn to them, he quickly climbed to the top to see what he could see. Still no friends. *What were they thinking to just leave and move on without me?* he thought. So he pressed on, moving swiftly, looking for any sign that would tell him where they were. After a significant period of time, he was beginning to wonder just where does this path lead? He knew he'd been wandering for a while but didn't know how long. He was hot, sweat was running down his face, dripping off his brow, and he was getting thirsty. Time seemed to be standing still. He noticed everything started to look the same, was his mind playing tricks on him? It seemed like it was the same cactus, the same rocks, the same big lizard he had recently passed, but it wasn't; he was on the same trail, moving farther away from the fork in the road with every step. Then all of a sudden, the trail just disappeared. *Oh great, now what do I do?* Out loud in controlled desperation, he said, "Lord, show me the way." Immediately his eyes fell on some cairns. He knew they were marking a path, but they were on the other side of the river.

Fear started pounding in his mind. *It's too dangerous; the water is too uncertain, you'll die if you try, don't do it, don't keep going, you don't know what lies ahead, whatever it is, it may kill you.* The fearful thoughts kept pounding and pounding relentlessly; it was becoming overwhelming. Finally, he screamed out to his mind, to the cloudless sky and everything around him, "No, in the name of Jesus, I rebuke that fear and cast it down...I am more than a conqueror; I am bold as a lion, I am a mighty man of valor, I am on an adventure! I will enjoy my time; I trust in You, Lord! There is somebody who needs me; I'm not the one lacking; I lack nothing, but I have everything to give...someone down the path needs what I have...I trust that You, Father, are with me ordaining my time, preparing my way."

Stopping on the bank, he took a few slow deep breaths to help calm himself down. Immediately he noticed the anxiety leave, and his whole body felt better; opening his eyes, he surveyed the water, looking for a suitable place to cross. The current was swift with the spring runoff, and he could see the outlines of rocks under the surface. Then his training kicked in. Long ago, when the boys were small, I had taught them how to read a river and choose a good place to cross no matter how swift or deep. Carefully picking his spot, he began to wade across the clear, blue-tinted water, navigating the rocks and current so as not to fall and get carried downstream. The water was flowing so fast that balancing barefoot on the rocks was an issue; it was also deeper than he wanted, but it was the shallowest place he could find. Determined to make it, he slowly and deliberately chose his steps and made it easily to the other side. In the Arizona heat, the cool water was actually very refreshing.

Finding a comfortable rock to rest on for a moment and get his bearings while he dried his feet and put his shoes back on, he noticed footprints and a heavily trafficked path. Looking back, he recognized the area and chose to move forward, still keenly aware of every sight and sound so as not to miss those friends that left him in the dust.

Pausing for a moment to take in the beautiful scenery, he gazed slowly across the rugged landscape and the layers of cliffs making up the canyon wall and the river that had carved its way beneath them. He had needed to calm himself again, to manage his emotions, to stay in control of his mind. Enjoying the world around him, the world outside of his mind, helped a lot. Breathing in deeply, he could smell the water, the willows, the cactus, the dirt, and the fragrant fresh air filled with the new spring growth popping out everywhere.

What an incredible place. "I'm supposed to be enjoying myself, but I think I'm lost," he mumbled to himself, "and the sun will be setting in about two hours." He had traveled a long time, since before noon, and still, no friends, not even another person had crossed his path. Again, fear started to filter in, and with it, a multitude of possible bad outcomes cascaded through his mind. Everything was dangerous; everything was fearful. *You can't find your way; no one knows you're here, and no one cares; you're probably going to die alone and lost in the desert.*

Taking authority over his mind, he said something similar to what he said before, "No, I don't accept that! No! No! I will make it back safely." He rebuked the fear in the name of Jesus and said out loud, "I am more than a conqueror; I am bold as a lion, I do not have the spirit of fear but love, power, and a sound mind; I am on an adventure! I will enjoy my time; I will trust the Lord! There is somebody who needs me. I'm not the one lacking. I lack nothing, but I have everything to give. Somebody down the path needs what I have. I trust that God is ordaining my time, preparing me..." Peace slowly but surely began to fill his mind. He could feel it like a blanket of warm honey that was pouring over him and through him. It felt wonderful, incredibly comforting, as it melted the fear and the torment from the vain imaginations away.

Feeling his confidence restored by the peace, he prayed, "Lord, send me the help I need, someone to show me the way." He had reached a point that he didn't know what else to do. Fifteen minutes later, he met a couple walking back to their kayak down at the river. It was an agonizingly long fifteen minutes, but somehow, he had a strong knowledge to just be patient his answer would come. So he had simply waited as he walked. He persevered, not knowing how long it would be.

He just believed.

They gave him water and showed him on a map where he was. Relieved, it was reassuring to see he was actually right where he needed to be. How nice; not only did the people have the answer about where he was, they shared their water with him, and they were glad to help. Garrett had come prepared; not only had his friends left him, but they had also taken his canteen and his snacks. Though the folks he met were just people, to him, they seemed like angels bringing answers and hope.

Refreshed by their kindness and their water Garrett watched as they made their way down the path back to the river, finally disappearing in the distance far below. He marveled that one minute he almost let himself panic, and the next, all was well, just because of a little knowledge and a little faith and a little patience. The knowledge was that he wasn't lost, he was on the right path, and all he had to do was follow it. His fear or lack of fear, his success or his failure in this situation was all in his mind. All anxiety, all concern, all the vain imaginations were now eliminated by the understanding that he was not lost. By knowing where he was, he was released from the torment that fear brings. Now the walk back was one of pure joy; he was going to enjoy every step, every sight, and every smell and sound. He could actually feel the joy welling up from inside of him, filling his whole being until it felt like it was oozing out of his pores.

Still marveling at how well things were turning out, he ran into one of the Indians on the path coming towards him. The young man stopped Garrett and said, "I have been watching for you to make sure you made it back safely; I could tell you thought you were lost." *Wow,* Garrett thought, *it's like this guy was a guardian angel looking out for me. Even if I had made a wrong turn, he would have come and found me and showed me the way home.* The Indian had been patiently watching from a high vantage point where he could see Garrett off and on throughout the day. He was waiting to see what he did, what choices he would make, and if he chose well or not, and if he didn't, the thoughtful young man was there to help. Isn't that a picture of God and how He helps us? His unconditional love for us?

To think that even if he had made the wrong choices that someone was there to help get him back on the right path was truly mind-boggling.

That's what God does for us, and all we have to do is ask. Wow.

He saw clearly that with that knowledge that someone was there watching over him, there never would have been a struggle in his mind because he would have known all along that he was going to be safe and taken care of. Fear could never have tormented him. And all of this was based on what he believed about his situation, and those beliefs then affected his thoughts. Isn't that what faith is all about? Believing in the better outcome even when it doesn't look like it's coming to pass?

Even though he chose well, he still had to control his mind, so fear didn't overtake him. The old adage that "knowledge is power" took on a whole new meaning. Just the knowledge that all was well, that he was headed in the right direction, gave him the mental power he needed to change his thinking. It gave him confidence; it gave him courage. Nothing changed in any of the circumstances around him. The only thing that changed for Garrett was his belief about those circumstances, all because of a little knowledge, which gave him the truth about where he really was. As his confidence then rose, it created a greater boldness, his faith grew stronger, and so did his understanding of what to say and what to do. He learned that sometimes things that look like dead ends aren't always dead ends.

As he enjoyed his long walk back, he thought about how well prepared he had been and how all that changed in a moment. He had his shirt, some water, his phone with a compass on it, and other things in his day pack, which one of the other guys was carrying. Yet the other guys ran off without thinking of the consequences of leaving Garrett alone all day long in the desert without any of his provisions, no water, and wearing only a pair of shoes and running shorts. The other guy had put a bunch of his stuff into the pack making it fairly heavy, and that's why Garrett had him carry it. He can carry his own junk; he had reasoned, a mistake he would never make again.

He considered that even with the best-laid plans, things could happen that change everything. Garrett was totally prepared, the others were not, yet they had his pack and everything he needed for a day in the desert. Now, what do you do? It's a good time to begin controlling your mind and your beliefs about your situation, separating what is really happening from what isn't happening, and making decisions with a clear head. These particular decisions all had to do with survival. Even though he went in and out of fear, Garrett didn't let himself panic, so he was able to control himself and make better decisions. He had to make adjustments based on the new facts and the circumstances that had changed in an instant and not freak out. He was now in the middle of a situation he hadn't counted on or even considered. He had been deserted. And by his own friends. That's not a contingency any of us would have considered.

Decisions made out of fear are not good, and decisions made out of panic are usually disastrous. Once he took control of his mind and spoke out some scriptures, the peace of God began to guard his thoughts, and life got better; he could think more clearly, decisions were easier. Looking at things through the filter of peace is always best. Though getting there isn't always easy and sometimes takes extreme mental control. But once you are in control of your mind and you're perceiving things through that filter of peace, the pressure of your circumstances isn't controlling you; you are managing the pressure. You are in control.

"Be anxious for nothing, but in everything by prayer and supplication with thanksgiving let your requests be made known to God. And the peace of God, which surpasses all comprehension, shall guard your hearts and your minds in Christ Jesus" (Philippians 4:6-7).

Who would have thought that a simple hike would turn into a life lesson on mind control, making decisions, relying on God for help, direction, and not letting fear control you?

What an incredible experience!
What a wonderful victory!
So are you wondering what happened?
When Garrett finally met up with the friends
who deserted him?

He beat the snot out of them!
Okay, so he didn't, but that's what he wanted to do. He had thought a lot about it as he wandered most of the day around the desert. But on the way back, just before the sunset, he forgave them. Once he did, all the animosity he had in his heart for them left, and he was totally loosed from them. Freedom! He just found out the hard way that they couldn't really be trusted; they weren't really the friends he thought they were.

And another thing that was just as big; he had to *forgive himself.*

The Wren and the Snake

Michelle and I were having our morning coffee under the large pine tree in our yard. Enjoying life, the view, and incredible place we live when the little wren, which is nesting in the birdhouse above us, landed on the hammock and started intensely rebuking us. Or so we thought.

The hammock is spread about six feet away on the other side of the tree. She was on the edge closest to us, franticly chattering and bouncing from side to side, making sounds that I had never heard before. She was so adamant that we both turned and just watched her. Her noisy rampage was totally interrupting our peace. She was used to us and usually just sat and sang while we relaxed under the tree. So this was pretty odd. Then I noticed she wasn't directing her call just at us; she was looking down, then back up at us like she was trying to say something, almost like she was trying to warn us. So I said to Michelle, "She's looking down; I wonder why?"

Then Michelle yells out, "Ah! It's a snake!"

Looking at the ground where the little bird was looking, I saw it, the back half of a large snake sprawled on the other side of the tree just a few feet from us. It was perfectly still. I quickly checked to see if it had a rattle; it didn't. *Good,* I thought, then figured out by its markings that it was a bull snake—a beneficial snake in these parts.

I ran and grabbed a shovel from the shed. Walking carefully to the other side of the tree so as not to spook it, I saw the snake; it was at least five feet long, had his head resting up about a foot off the ground against the tree, and was so focused on the little wren that he didn't even notice me. He wanted that bird for breakfast and was poised to strike if it would just get a little closer.

Quickly putting the shovel under part of his outstretched body, I tried to throw him away from us. But no luck. He slipped off my shovel and slithered around the tree, through the holly and the rocks towards Michelle. She squealed and jumped backward, right out of the chair. (Quite a move if I do say so myself.) Suddenly he saw her and stopped, not sure where to go. Trying in vain to throw him again with the shovel without hurting him, he got away and crawled into a small hole under a rock near our chairs. He was harmless. Heck, I wanted him to keep eating all the little critters that want to come into our house. I knew that after we left, he would slither away, and we'd probably never see him again, so I wasn't worried.

We finished our coffee and marveled at how the little wren warned us so fearlessly of impending danger. We looked up, following the sound of her beautiful song. She was peacefully stretching out her wing, preening herself as she sang on a branch near her nest. Perfectly safe and content, now that I had removed the danger. It was as though she was thankful to me for helping her. Yes, life is good!

God speaks to us in so many different ways that I think that sometimes we don't realize it is actually Him. It's not for us to decide how He should speak and what means He should use. It's for us to decide to simply listen, no matter how He chooses to speak. So what was He saying this time? That He cares about all His creation, even down to the needs of a little bird. Like it is written, if He cares so for the birds, how much more does He care for us? How much more does He love us?

We sat and pondered those things aloud, marveling together at God's goodness until our attention was diverted by the doe with three fawns. About thirty yards away, the triplets, still sporting their spots, were sniffing and snorting and frolicking around as they worked their way into the meadow in front of us. Morning coffee at our house is never boring. God loves us. And God cares for all His creation. Yes, life is good!

Witches Outside

I worked for about a year in the prayer center of a large international ministry. My shift started at 3:45 a.m., so I had to leave the house around 3 a.m. every morning. It was interesting; we never knew where the next call would be from, the Caribbean, Canada, the United States, or the United Kingdom and Europe. Every request you can imagine came across our desks; intense, desperate, humorous, sad, tragic, and praise reports. God always came through in some way, and it was amazing to hear how He had worked.

One morning I wasn't particularly awake as I stumbled through the motions of preparing for my day. I needed to go out to start the car to let it warm up on the chilly winter night. Stepping onto the front porch, I took a deep breath, braced myself for the cold, and noticed there was a man-sized, dark hooded figure hovering about three feet off the ground to my right, about ten feet away. It was over the grass just outside of the porch. *Hum, that's pretty odd. I must not be awake yet because I'm seeing things,* was all I thought. The ice on the ground crunched loudly under my feet as I walked to the car. Looking up over the car, the door was creaking from the cold as it opened; I see there are twelve more hooded figures standing silently on the sidewalk across the street. No movement, no sound. I turn and look to see if the first one was still hovering in one place over the yard. Yep, still there. My next thought was, "Well, that's strange." So I closed my eyes for a moment then looked back across the street. Yep, still there, all twelve of them too. Then I looked back at hover dude; yep, he was still there too. Well, I thought, I guess they're real. Going back into the house, I finish my coffee, thinking that it will help me see straight, then I slowly open the front door to peek out. They were all still there. *Weird*, I thought to myself.

I determine now I'm going to get Michelle out of bed and get her to the front door to see if she sees them too. I mean, am I really seeing these things, or am I still not quite awake? It is 3 a.m., you know. Stopping in my tracks in the middle of the living room, I realize that if she does see these things, and then I leave, she might get scared, so I'll wait to tell her when we're both awake; I reason to myself.

By now, I was much more awake and starting to be bothered by what I could see. After taking a sip of a new cup of coffee, my mind had begun to clear up enough to know the darn things were spirits. So stepping back out on the porch into the frigid, black night, I bound them and cast them away in the name of Jesus. And nothing happened. They didn't budge; they didn't make a sound. So I said it again, and again nothing happened.

This was not good, not good at all. Now, what do I do, Lord? I had to leave for work, but I didn't want to leave my family unprotected, especially from something evil lurking outside that I could see, and others probably couldn't. So I sealed the spirits and our home with the blood of Jesus, got in my car, and left. I couldn't have gone except that I had this strong peace upon me that my family would be okay and realized I wasn't bothered anymore, which felt really good. But this was definitely weird. I've seen and experienced spiritual things all of my life, even before I became a Christian. I just like to make sure it's not my mind or my imagination playing tricks on me. I always verify if it's real. And this? This was real.

As I prayed in the Spirit, I heard inside me that still small voice; He said they were witches, and they were there to curse me and my family but not to worry because they can't touch us. "For greater is He that is in us than he that is in them" (1 John 4:4). Okay, so does that mean that human spirits don't respond the same to the name of Jesus as evil spirits? He just said that the evil in them couldn't touch us.

At work, I told some folks about it, wondering if they had any insight into this mystery, and they responded with the same thing. They are witches, human spirits. How can they do that? I asked. Nobody knew. We were all still a bit naive about some spiritual things. But we were learning quickly. As always, God took care of all the things we had no clue about.

It was a short time later when I got a good answer from an ex-warlock. Astral projection was his answer. He said they used to do it all the time. They couldn't ever touch Christians though he said something more powerful than them was always guarding them, keeping them safe. Many times they would see an untouchable bright light, or angels, huge, mighty ones, guarding the people or their property, and they couldn't go past them. They were also incredibly fearsome to look at and many times caused the witches to be so scared they would have to leave…quickly. Other times there would be some kind of barrier, sometimes they could see it, and sometimes they couldn't, but either way, they never were able to pass it. Hummm…interesting answer.

Every morning for the next couple of weeks or so, when I stepped outside to go to work, there they were, silently standing there. Or, in the case of the one near the house, just hovering there above the ground. So I always spoke to them something like, "I seal my family and my home with the blood of Jesus; you cannot touch or harm them in any way. I break your power and all your plans with the blood of Jesus, and I say we are safe from you or anything associated with you in Jesus' name. Now be gone!"

Then I would get in my car and drive to work. The first few days, it was weird, really weird, and I didn't want to leave, but then this special peace would wrap around me, and it was the Lord letting me know all was fine; I didn't need to be concerned. After a while, I got so used to them being there I'd run out the door, hold up my hand towards them, and quickly rebuke them and all they were trying to do in the name of Jesus. I had already sealed my family and all we have with the blood of Jesus, so I didn't need to do it again. It felt like when I did this that it tormented them, and I loved tormenting them.

For some reason, it seemed their resolve against me was strong, I never knew their plan or purpose, but obviously, it wasn't good; I mean, the devil comes to steal, kill and destroy, and they work for him. After a while, their power began to wane, and so did their resolve, and the weaker they got, the more transparent they got until one night they were gone. I never saw them again.

We found out later that satanic rituals were performed at our house, and a witch's coven had lived there at some time in the past. That explained the demonic activity. When we first moved in, we were constantly casting out evil spirits and being bothered by an evil presence. It was very annoying. So we went around the house and property anointing it with the blood of Jesus, and that pretty much got rid of the torment from those spirits there.

The kids loved doing it; they were four, six, and seven years old. We'd give them each a glass of water. (An unbreakable plastic glass.) Pray over it that it was a representation of the blood of Jesus, then turn them loose. They'd sprinkle it on everything that water wouldn't hurt, the walls, the floor, the ceiling, each other, and every time they'd flick it with their fingers, they'd say, "The blood of Jesus, the blood of Jesus, I anoint this with the blood of Jesus, no evil can cross this bloodline." It always worked well and showed them that even little kids can use the power of the blood and have good results. Age doesn't matter. And besides, they had all seen and experienced the evil at this house, so why shouldn't they get to be a part of getting rid of it? We learned a lot about the incredible power of the blood of Jesus here. Turns out there's a number of barriers the spirits and witches can't cross, but the blood of Jesus seems to be the most powerful.

I wish I could say that with a word, the witches were gone. They weren't. But I can say that with a word, all their power was bound, and their devices were broken and removed. We learned here how to stand continually in faith in the Word and that it was working whether we were thinking about it or not. That it's also working when we're working, when we're playing, when we're eating or just relaxing or sleeping or watching TV simply because it's always working, and so is your faith.

(Look in Isaiah 54 and Mark 11 about the words you speak.) Either you believe for things to happen according to the scriptures you are standing on, or you believe for the worst and for bad things to happen by your worry. You're going to believe something, so it might as well be the something that helps and doesn't hinder, especially when witches are trying to curse you. Sometimes things are so intense you can't afford to worry; you don't want to bring destruction down on your own head.

You can talk about the problems without worrying about them, and you can discuss all the situations without letting fear take over. You just don't want to dwell on the problems; you want to dwell on the solutions. You just have to believe in your prayers and the scriptures you are basing them on. God will take care of the rest. You just have to believe, as Jesus said to Jairus when things looked so bad for him and his little dying daughter, "Do not be afraid, just believe" (Luke 8:50, NIV). No, it isn't easy, but then again, it is. Sometimes, especially when you first start to live this way, it feels like such a paradox. With practice, you can have better control over your mind, and things will improve. That's the starting place, your mind.

When I finally asked my wife and kids if anyone could see the spirits, no one could. I was relieved; I think that was best. I think if they could have seen them, they would have struggled with fear. So I'm glad they couldn't see anything this time. It was God's grace.

Speaking these scriptures out loud with your family in situations like this is also very powerful and makes a difference for you:

Psalm 18

Psalm 59

Psalm 64

Psalm 91

I always get results when I do this.

The flower in this picture is in a pond nearby.

A Place to Pray

We all need a place to pray, a private place, a place where we won't be interrupted, where we can spend time not just praying but listening for answers too, whether it's in our easy chair, our bedroom, the kitchen, an office, or while we're walking or riding a horse. For us, our favorite place is a beautiful, secluded spot we call the prayer meadow that we go to when the weather allows.

Crow Convention

One day in the summer, while Michelle was working in the yard, she heard this loud noise that reminded her of mass confusion. *What! Where's that coming from?* she thought, *and what the heck is it?* Looking up toward the sound, she was astonished.

There were so many crows flying low overhead that they darkened the sky. They were headed for the cliff right behind our house.

She went and stood on the deck in the back and just marveled at what she saw. The crows had all landed on the rocks, so many of them that the cliff looked like it was alive and moving. A huge, weird, black mass of life moving in its own odd rhythm. And the noise! The sound was deafening; it was so loud she couldn't even hear herself think, and not only that, it was echoing all the way down the meadow. Wow, what a sight, what a sound. And it wasn't just part of the cliff that was covered; it was the whole thing, the whole side of the mountain.

It didn't take long, and she began to feel bothered, even tormented like something bigger and more ominous than the crows had settled in and was taking over.

It was odd, but Michelle was at the point of feeling overwhelmed. Then a scripture about the power in Jesus' name flashed into her mind (Acts 3:16), and this righteous indignation rose up within her, and she screamed at the top of her lungs, "I command every bird that is not of God, every crow that has witchcraft working in it to leave now in Jesus' name! Go! Go! Go! Now in Jesus' name!"

So, you want to know what happened?

Three quarters of the crows just flew away. She watched, and they just kept flying and disappeared off in the distance. The crows that were left on the rocks quieted down and began to go about their business, and peace returned. *Wow,* she thought, *the power of God is big, really big, and not only that, it works, it really works!* God is definitely not in the box we had kept him in by what we believe and don't believe that He can do.

And what about dominion? Who would have thought we actually had dominion over things in creation? (Genesis 1:28). This definitely messed with our belief system. I guess we'll just have to believe that what the Bible said is true. We'll have to just believe.

Just a side note; not every crow is evil or has witchcraft working in it. Only some of them do, and then only sometimes. We don't need to be afraid of them or constantly suspicious. Besides, who created the crows? God did, and crows are not inherently evil. He created them for a purpose, a good purpose. Why can witchcraft sometimes work through them? I don't know, it sometimes does, and when it does, we just take care of it by the power of Jesus' name, and you can too.

Do we also go around commanding all the animals what to do? No, that's not our place. The Father does a much better job of that than we ever could. Though I must admit, I do command, in Jesus' name, the skunks to go where I can't smell them and the screech owls to go where I can't hear them. I draw the line of intervention at torment or danger.

Arthritis

I love this story. Early one morning at the prayer center, I answered a call from an older woman with arthritis pain throughout her body. I had asked her what exactly she wanted me to pray for. "Well, son," she answered, "the pain is so bad I can't move at all today, so I need the pain to go away, and I'd like to be healed from this."

"Okay, ma'am, just listen then as I pray, and we'll agree that the Lord will not only take away the pain but heal you also. Is that okay with you?"

"Oh yes," she replied. I could feel the excitement and expectancy coming through the phone line.

"Father, I pray for healing for this woman. I break this curse of arthritis from her body, and I speak life over her from her head to her toes. May you move through her whole body and remove all of the arthritis from her blood and her bones, and I command the pain to be gone and never return in Jesus' name. Okay, ma'am, how do you feel, is the pain gone or diminished yet? How do your fingers feel?"

"Well, I can see that it's twenty till 10 a.m." *What!* I thought to myself, *We're praying for arthritis, and she's telling me the time.*

Looking towards the clock on the wall, I see it's twenty till 9; she's in a different time zone than we are.

"Ma'am, my clock says twenty till also, but I was hoping your pain had decreased or even disappeared. Do you still have any pain?"

"I can see the clock," she said excitedly.

Great, I thought to myself, another crazy person. Now, what do I do?

"No, you don't understand," she said, talking and sobbing at the same time. "I've been blind for years, but now I can see."

"Really?" I said, shocked and not knowing what to think.

"You see," she went on, "not only could I not see the time; I couldn't even see the clock on the wall. I can see, I can see!" she yelled out, no longer sobbing. "Thank you, thank you, I have my life back, thank you!"

I was so surprised I couldn't think of anything to say for a few moments. "Wow, I'm praying about arthritis; I don't even know you're blind, and Jesus takes a prayer for pain and opens your eyes."

"Amazing, Jesus truly is amazing." She spent the next few minutes praising Jesus. I just sat and listened quietly on the other end of the phone, enjoying her victory with her as her joy not only filled her home, but it began spilling over into the prayer center, too—what an incredible experience. God is constantly taking Himself out of whatever box I have Him in. I don't think I've ever heard more thankfulness in my whole life as I heard that day. You know, it's one thing to read about it in the Bible; it's another thing to actually experience it yourself. It changes everything you believe. Jesus really does open the eyes of the blind.

Caught in the Changing Tide

Our friend, Gin, found the perfect beach for us to sit and enjoy the ocean, life, and the California sun. Eric, her husband, was working, but the kids, Mason, and Erica were with us. It was early fall, and school had started, so there really weren't that many people there to compete for our little spot in the sand. I was enjoying the young teenagers frolicking in the shallow water and riding skimboards. Man, that looked fun.

Sizing up the waves, we decided to go for a swim. The surf was easy, and the waves beyond were rolling pleasantly until they crested then crashed effortlessly just beyond the beach. Erica was the only one that would join us; Gin was satisfied watching from her comfortable seat in the sand. Like always, the water was on the cold side, but once in it, you get used to it fairly quickly. Once we were waist-deep, we all dove in just to get it over with and not be tortured by the cold any longer.

Moving slowly a little farther outward to where we couldn't touch bottom any longer, we treaded water together; it was eight to ten feet deep, the girls were chattering happily, it was a good day to be alive.

Suddenly we notice Gin is standing up, yelling and motioning frantically for us to come in. Mason is standing nearby, as are the few others there that day, and they are all looking out in our direction. We saw Jaws, so our only thought is that there is a shark, and we need to come in. The noise of the surf kept us from hearing what anyone was trying to say. I look to both sides of me to see if I can see any fins or other signs of a shark and notice that Michelle and Erica have both suddenly drifted too far away from me. Not good. I focus on Mason and then Gin trying to discern what they are trying to communicate, but because of my filter from Jaws, all I can figure out is that there's a shark, and we need to come in quickly. Looking again at Erica and Michelle, I am shocked that they are both gone. I look again—still no sight of them. I look at the water again for fins or blood hoping it's not true and that they are okay—nothing, nothing at all. My heart sank with sadness and despair for them, and then panic started to pound me.

Then I caught myself. *What if it isn't a shark? What if it's something else, and all this is only in my mind?* Torn by the thoughts of extreme danger and tragedy and the wonder of what is true, I notice a large wave starting to crash down on top of me. I react by immediately going underwater so it can go over me and I can come up on the other side. But it's bigger than I know, and it pushes me clear to the bottom and rolls me like a rag doll until I don't know which way is up. I'm out of breath and open my eyes while I let myself begin to float to see which way is up. I feel myself rising and notice a patch of blue above the water and shoot towards it. Breaking the surface with incredible relief, I gasp for air as another huge wave slams me back down to the bottom, rolling me again until its strength is spent, and so is mine. In my mind, I was saying over and over again, *Jesus, Jesus, help me, Jesus.* The situation had become desperate, and I wasn't going to make it without some help. Feeling it let up enough so I can climb for air, I again barely see the patch of blue and use every ounce of strength to make it back to the surface.

The panic I felt earlier and the strength I had used to just survive left my body so weak I could hardly reach the surface. Three or four gasps of air, and oh no, another huge wave is thrusting me helplessly to the bottom and dragging me across the sand. I used to swim and dive, and holding my breath was nothing. But now I'm out of shape and overweight and in no condition for this kind of abuse. *Oh, Jesus, help me, I'm not going to die like this,* I said in my mind as I was being pushed along the bottom again. I went into survival mode. It didn't matter what I could or couldn't do; I was going to live no matter what, no matter how long I had to be thrown about or hold my breath.

No longer being dragged uncontrollably along, I made myself head for the little patch of blue that was my salvation. Breaking the surface again, prepared but not ready for another wave, I breathed massive amounts of air as deep and quickly into my lungs as I could. Thankfully the next waves were easy to navigate, and I just floated and filled my body with air. Looking for Erica or Michelle, I still don't see them; even the shore is just an occasional glimpse between the up and down of the large swells.

I knew if I didn't make it to shore now that I would die, so I determined to do whatever it would take to make it in. The only thing moving my arms and legs was the strength of my will. I didn't have the strength left in my muscles to swim, and I still hadn't completely caught my breath.

I just knew there was no way I was going to die now, and whatever it took, I would make it to the shore. *Jesus, help me!* I said again in my mind. My next memories are a jumble of waves crashing over me, above water, below water, and finally to a place where I could feel the bottom with my knees. I don't know how I made it; one minute, I was a painfully long way from the beach, in deeper water, praying for help; the next, I was in shallow water crawling forward on my knees. Somehow the Lord got me back to safety. The waves were still tossing me to and fro, but at least I was kind of on solid ground as I crawled and scooted with the rhythm of the flow of the water towards the shore.

Heaving from holding my breath so long and pulling myself up to dry ground was probably the hardest thing I've ever done in my life. Still on my knees, I tried to stand numerous times but couldn't, I knew if I did, I would fall over, so I quit trying. I just felt so weak and so shaky, so I waited for what seemed like a very long time until I felt more strength beginning to flow through my body and decided that no matter what it took, I would stand and not fall and walk to my chair in the sand. My muscles weren't responding well, but somehow, I just stood up even though everything within me was screaming, *I can't!* Then I slowly and deliberately moved one foot in front of the other until I collapsed into the chair. Everything was in pain, my muscles, my lungs, even my brain. Focusing my eyes back on the pounding surf, I struggle to hold my head up and search first for Michelle, then Erica, knowing that even if I saw one of them, there was nothing I could do about it. It was the first time in my life where I was actually helpless, and it felt disgustingly miserable. I felt for a moment ashamed that I was in such bad shape. Still looking for shark fins, I look for any sign of life to give me hope, thinking someone may have fallen victim. I still didn't get it that the danger was the waves; it was never from a shark. I wasn't thinking clearly, yet I was still in survival mode. But thank God I had survived.

Erica had been beaten by the three waves also, and on the last one, she went down and couldn't get back up. In her mind, she cried out, *Oh, God, I have to breathe. I have to get a breath of air; please help me.* It didn't matter if it was above water or still under the water; she was simply going to breathe. As she slowly began to open her mouth, a hand came out of nowhere and pulled her up by her hair. It was a female lifeguard that had seen the spot where she disappeared and reached into the churning water and found her a few feet below the surface. Spitting and sputtering, she fought for those first few precious breaths of air. Then the lifeguard quickly got her to shore and to safety. She just sat there for quite a while, stunned at what just happened and trying to process it all.

Michelle had thought it odd that we just disappeared. She thought we had been eaten by the shark and that she was probably next. None of us realized until afterward that the currents had quickly changed and become so strong that they had pulled us apart. A strong rip tide had formed. The sets of waves had changed and gotten dangerous for us, and we had no clue; we didn't know that such a thing could even happen so quickly.

Michelle's fear, thinking about the shark and that we weren't there because we'd been eaten, turned to panic as she flailed around trying to stay afloat. Then the first wave crashed on her head and drove her under the water. Finally able to come back to the surface, she gets a breath, and another wave hits her and holds her down. Shocked that this is all happening so suddenly and unable to get a good breath, she panics even more. As she comes up, she starts furiously swimming towards the beach and trying to breathe, but another wave pounds her and holds her down again. Now she's not trying to swim; she's struggling to survive, to just breathe, to just stay above the water. Then the next wave hits, pushing her under again. Panic had now taken over as she fought to the surface again. Now the panic and the struggle had drained her of any strength she had left; she wasn't able to move; she was so exhausted that keeping her head above water seemed impossible. Her only focus now was breathing and survival. She thought this was it; she was going to die. *Jesus, help me,* was going through her mind.

At that very moment, a young man, a lifeguard, popped up in front of her and said, "Are you okay?"

She sheepishly answered, "Yes, I'm okay."

Then he said, "There's another wave; go down, down, down," then pushed her head underwater as the wave rolled over the top of them. She popped back up, sputtering, and he said, "Do you need my help?"

In desperation, she said, "Yes!"

He put a life vest over her head and said, "Kick your feet." He started to swim fast and easily toward the shore. Relief began flooding her soul. One moment she's dying; the next, she's being rescued. She just let him tow her; she had no strength left to kick her feet.

Once at the beach, she could hardly move. Standing up to get out of the water was almost impossible, so she sat at the edge of the water with Erica as they recounted each other's brush with death and recuperated from the ordeal. Walking to her beach chair was difficult, and she felt very embarrassed as she sat down totally exhausted. Embarrassed that she could not save herself that she had to be rescued, but so thankful to be safe now. Thankful to be alive.

Who would have thought that something as simple as floating in the water could have turned into a tragedy? Jesus saved all three of us that day. He saved us from what we didn't know, and He saved us from what we couldn't do. I believe that if we hadn't called out to Him each in our own way that we all might have died that day. Thank God we all know Him, and we all cried out to Him when we most needed His help. Thank God He answered our calls at just the right moment.

Sometimes in other areas of life, things change like the tide, and we have no clue and don't know what to do. But the Lord does. The Lord knows how to guide us and deliver us no matter the circumstances. We just need to cry out to Him and then believe He will help us as we do what we know to do.

And don't give up!

Close Encounters of the Wrong Kind

Ever since we had been married, about fifteen years at that time, Michelle had trouble with random men coming out of nowhere and trying to hurt her or following her with obvious evil intent. At first, it was annoying for me; then, it got scary. It's one thing to hear about it, which is bad enough, but it's a whole other thing to actually see it happen before your eyes.

I got used to the Holy Spirit telling me to pray so that something bad doesn't happen to Michelle. I never knew what to pray, so I just prayed in the Spirit until I felt a release. Sometimes it was short, just seconds, and sometimes it seemed to take forever, but I always went until I had the breakthrough, I had a treasure (my wife) that needed protecting, and I knew beyond a shadow of doubt that my prayers worked, that the Lord was in them. Sometimes she would come home with a story of deliverance, and other times, not. The not's meant that whatever Satan had planned against her didn't happen, and she was safe.

I was in Florida at Christian International for a business-men's retreat. While they were playing the preliminary worship, I had this overwhelming urge to tell this lady in front of me about the situation with Michelle. I'd never seen her before and didn't know her name, but the Holy Spirit wouldn't let up. So I finally gave in, quit wondering what she would think of my strange request, and tapped her on the shoulder and gave a very short version of what had been going on.

I said to her, "Ma'am, the Holy Spirit said you would have an answer for me."

She very graciously answered, "Well, tell me the question." So, I told her about Michelle constantly being stalked and almost attacked not just in secluded areas but in public places by weird demonic men.

Here are a few instances, like this guy at the grocery store. I dropped Michelle off to pick up donuts for a class we were attending at church. As she was chatting with the clerk, she had that odd feeling you get when you can feel someone staring at you. Looking over the register, she noticed a man hidden behind a display except for his eyes; her first thought was, *How weird if looks could kill, I'd be dead.* He gave her the creeps. She looked away then back again to see if he was still there. She could see him now, and he had that "I'm going to get you and rape you and I hate you" look. And he was incessantly flipping his keys. She knew I was going to pull up to the front as soon as I saw her come out, so she figured if he followed her, she would start screaming to scare him away and let others know what was going on while she ran to our van. He never took his eyes off of her, which creeped her out even more, and as soon as she passed near where he was lurking, she noticed that he waited just a moment, then quickly got right behind her and was following her step by step out of the door.

Seeing I was nearby and already coming to pick her up, she stopped in the busy, large open doorway and waited for a few very long scary moments for me to get there. The creepy guy had stopped directly behind her; she could hear him and feel his sinister presence there. As she opened the door and literally jumped in, he moved forward towards her like he was going to grab her then stopped himself, staring with a wild animal look in his eyes and seething with such hatred that it was oozing out of him, all while violently flipping his keys in his hand. We all saw him at that point, the kids were amazed as they could see and feel the hatred, too, and they all commented, "Wow, Mom, that man is evil, and he was going to get you if we hadn't pulled up." It scared them for her; they wanted to protect her and go beat him up. Needless to say, we had a great discussion afterward about evil people and what are the different things you can do if someone is after you, and how the Lord had every piece of the puzzle in order for Michelle's safety, escape and victory. The boys were about thirteen, twelve, and ten.

Before we were married, an ex-boyfriend came to the house she shared with her sister and began beating her. He was crazy, extremely jealous, and a controller; that's why he was an "ex" boyfriend. She tried to run, but he chased her and trapped her in the bathroom, hitting her so hard it knocked her through the shower door, breaking it, as she fell into the bathtub. "I'm going to hurt you so bad and mangle your face so that no one will ever want you," he proclaimed proudly. He said that if he couldn't have her, then he'd make it so no one could." But the Holy Spirit gave her a clever ploy, and she miraculously got away to the safety of a neighbor's house.

It all started when she was little. Michelle had a number of men that tried to get her into their cars; first, they would ask, then when she wouldn't comply, they would get mad and try to force her. Every time she would run and get away.

The same thing happened to our youngest, Bryce, many times, which was very alarming to us. The disturbing thing is these men, and it was always men, would sometimes hunt him down relentlessly for hours while he ran and hid over and over while making his way strategically towards our home. But the Lord always hid him and showed him where to go next, and he was never harmed. He learned how to recognize the Lord's voice during these intense times and to follow it. The same spirit that tried to destroy Michelle was now trying to destroy our son. It had passed to the next generation. No matter how we prayed, it never got rid of this torment of evil men trying to harm them; it just kept happening, though it did diminish. But the Lord always protected them and showed them what to do to evade and escape. Can you imagine as a little kid or a woman having to deal with this harrowing stuff all the time?

Another time Michelle and one of our sons that she was homeschooling were making their way to the car in the parking lot. He was following with the cart full of food, and she was a couple of cars ahead. Looking up across the lot, she saw a man coming straight towards her with blood on the front of his shirt and down his sleeves. He was gritting his teeth, breathing heavily and growling slightly, like an animal. When she saw him, she thought, *He's coming after me*. Then stopped and questioned

Error

 134

herself thinking, *Oh, surely not.* Looking up again, it was pretty obvious he was headed right for her. She stopped and watched him for a moment as she was deciding what to do, then, all of a sudden, he turned and headed the other way. Everything about him was incredibly eerie in a surreal sort of way. It was like he had come straight out of a horror movie. Garrett had reached her by then and yelled out, "Mom, did you see that guy?"

"Yes," she replied, watching to see where he went.

Garrett continued, "Mom, he was after you!"

She asked, "Do you really think he was?"

"Yes! he was coming right at you, then he saw me and turned away."

Michelle told him that's what she thought too and that she was glad he was with her and also saw it happen. Because others might not believe it, it seemed too weird to be true.

Back in Florida, the nice lady asked, "What is your wife's name?" And then said, "Give me your hands." So I placed my hands in hers; she closed her eyes and prayed simply, "Lord, show me about Michelle." She began by saying, "Two, three, no, four generations back, a woman in her immediate family line was raped and murdered. That spirit has followed the family line down to her." So she prayed that it would be bound and stop tormenting her in Jesus' name. Then she said, "The Lord said to have the pastor's wife where we go to church pray specifically for this."

I was so relieved to hear the simple truth. "Thank you, ma'am, and by the way, what's your name?"

"Mary, Mary Crumb," she replied with a twinkle in her eye.

A number of weeks went by with no incidents of any trouble whatsoever. We were so relieved. It was incredible. Michelle had never experienced such freedom from men coming against her in her life; it was obvious God had moved and answered Mary's prayer. Then she said it was starting up again, she was worried, now what do we do? We were reminded that she hadn't completed her part of the task.

Cheryl, the pastor's wife, had women's prayer early in the morning once a week. Michelle usually went and loved it; the times of prayer were powerful. So she caught Cheryl at a time she could listen, told her a brief version of the story and how this other woman had said to have her pray for Michelle.

Cheryl acted like she didn't want to and like her prayer really wouldn't matter but said, "Well, okay, be set free from this in Jesus' name." Then she tapped Michelle on the shoulder and turned and walked away. At first, Michelle was disappointed at her attitude; then, she decided not to take any offense, roll it over on God and simply believe that the prayer, no matter how it was given, would work. And you know what? That was many years ago, and the torment has not come against her since. It worked.

Even though the pastor's wife didn't think it mattered, it still worked. Amazingly it worked despite her unbelief. And you know what else? From the moment Michelle was prayed for, Bryce was set free from the same torment. Never again did he have men coming after him to harm him. Who would have thought that breaking a generational curse over Michelle was the answer to setting Bryce free and removing that spirit from our family line forever?

Wow, the Lord and the words we speak are so much more powerful than we can even imagine, even when we don't know if we can believe them, even when we doubt. Amazing, don't you think? Not only that, but look what a little insight from the Lord did. It told us what the problem was and how to take care of it, and nothing we had to do was difficult; it was simple, and it changed our lives for the better.

I'd like to address something else that helped our family in these threatening situations. Of course, we had the "how to deal with strangers" talk. But because of these and other things coming against us, we were forced to deal in depth with how to evade, resist, and escape. And actually, go over various scenarios in little kid language so they could understand what to do. For our kids, these things were fun for them to talk about. We also practiced "situational awareness" when we were out and about, so they would be more aware of what's really going on around them. They were all already having to use what we taught them, and it was saving their lives. They were young, only four, six, and seven. How sad that they were having to deal with these things at such a young age, and how wonderful that we were able to train them to not only survive but to prevail.

Aside from performing His Word, the Lord expects us to use some common sense too.

Many things can be avoided by simply using common sense.

Complacency can be deadly.

And situational awareness is always important.

Psalm 59, 64, and 91. We speak these scriptures and others out regularly, as a couple and as a family, and agree together for many difficult situations, and it always works.

Rattlesnake

I killed a rattlesnake.

Michelle and I had been up in the meadow praying, and we were walking down the path towards the house. Irises and poppies were in bloom everywhere. We were collecting different colored ones so Michelle could put them in a vase on our windowsill. Suddenly the mountain quiet was broken by the distinct rattling of a snake. He was obviously nearby, but we couldn't see him. I eased down the path towards the sound, looking for the snake that had interrupted the peaceful afterglow from our time with God.

There he was.

Curled up beside the path angrily rattling, coiled, and ready to strike.

He was over three feet long. Big for this area.

When it is in my power, I never leave something dangerous that would harm others.

I eliminate the threat.

Quickly noticing absolutely nothing to adequately kill him with, I decided to go the thirty yards to the house and get the shovel.

I told Michelle to keep his attention while I got the shovel.

"Don't let him get away," I admonished.

"What! Don't let him get away?"

How the heck am I supposed to keep a snake from getting away, and how am I supposed to keep his attention? she thought.

Stepping slowly around him just out of striking range, I noticed his head following my every move. It actually turned with me so he could look right at me. Hmmm, I never had one do that before.

Grabbing the shovel and hurrying back up the path, I see Michelle standing like a statute, barely moving the things in her hand.

"He's been watching for you ever since you left. Waiting for you to come back," she said.

She didn't want to be too obvious to the snake. She didn't want him coming after her. She thought he might jump at her or chase her or something. That's why she decided not to keep his attention but just watch him.

She tried.

She did it afraid, but at least she did it. At least he didn't get away.

When he saw me again, his rattling was recharged to a fever pitch.

He rose up, getting ready to strike.

I stepped to just the right distance to attack and still be safe.

Holding the shovel with both hands towards the end of the handle, I taunted him with the back of the spade.

As he struck, I lifted it up, so his head and that part of his body shot underneath.

Then before he could snap back, I brought the blade down hard.

Severing his head from his body. (This ain't my first rodeo.)

His head jumped up and down as his jaws opened and shut, still trying to bite.

Then taking the still whipping, slivering body, I cut off the rattle and threw the remains into the bushes. Another animal will eat well tonight.

Victory!

See, the Lord showed me that as we walk the path of life. Even after praying and spending time with Him that Satan, the old serpent whose purpose is to kill, steal, and destroy, is sometimes waiting in ambush for us. But if we confront as we are confronted with or without fear, then we win. Sure works better without fear because we move without the hindrance of false perceptions. A false perception, in this case, is like seeing through the filter of fear which can cause us to make bad choices, deadly choices.

Faith brings confidence
and confidence boldness,
and boldness brings courage
and all together, they bring victory.

I also saw how when we are ready in season and out that we prevail.

We attack the attacker from a place of power,

being trained and prepared well enough that we think clearly,

we move with purpose, and all that we do is effective.

His incredible love for us,

His amazing protection,

the power in His name, the name of Jesus.

His Word that always accomplishes what it is sent to do and never returns void.

His anointing that causes us to win and breaks every yoke.

When we live and walk in this revelation, how can we fail?

With a sound mind, we assess the situation,

take the weapons at hand (because we are well versed in them all).

Cut off his head and take his tail for plunder.

Victory is truly sweet.

Sometimes we just don't realize the power of our words,

or the power in the name of Jesus.

As it is written:

"My people die for lack of knowledge."

What's your Sign?

My grandfather "Lu" Holland was a young cowboy when he first came to Colorado. His specialty was breaking horses. He would hire on with an outfit or a ranch and work with the untrained horses. Once they were all broke and fit to ride, his job was over, and he would move on to the next outfit. He worked his way across Texas and Oklahoma, even working at his favorite outfit, The 101, for a season before ending up in Denver sometime around 1906, give or take a few years.

At this point, he could see the days of the carefree cowboy as he knew them were beginning to end; the west was changing more every year, so he turned in his saddle and spurs for a French knife and a chef's hat. Training under the ole German chefs at the Brown Palace, he spent a number of years there perfecting his new craft. Once earning the title of Chef, he struck out on his own again, opening a restaurant just a few blocks away. It was called the Pine Grove, where during the roaring '20s, you paid a nickel to listen to the band and got your lunch for free.

Fast forward years later to the Holland House in Golden, our family hotel and restaurant that he bought during World War II, where I asked him why he put up the arch. He spoke of his travels while breaking horses and how miserable he felt when he'd come across people who were suspicious, indifferent, judgmental, or even rude when entering a new town or area. To this day, he said he would never go back to such a place because of the bad impression those people had left him with. On the other hand, everywhere he went where he was welcomed in a pleasant manner made him feel wonderful. He said it seemed somehow the sun shined brighter in those places. A smile crossed his face, and his eyes went glassy as he paused for a moment remembering those special places from so long ago.

Somewhere along that road, after a violent, deadly encounter with a mad man and his six-shooter, Granddad said, "This weary traveling cowboy determined in his heart to make a special point of always offering a friendly 'Welcome' to other fellow travelers." He called it the first part of Western Hospitality. So once he had established himself in Golden, he decided he was in a place to do something about that promise he'd made to himself long ago, *to welcome all travelers and passers-by.*

He wanted something that might inspire Western Hospitality among Goldenites and, more importantly, give even the weariest of travelers the comfort of knowing that they were truly "welcome" in this place.

How could such a thing be accomplished, something that would actually work and be consistent, any time for anyone?

The arch was his answer, an arch that spanned the main street that you would go under as you enter town. That way, he could put a concise and simple message proclaiming to one and all that they are valuable and precious to us, and we're glad that they are here. So, this is what it says:

WELCOME TO GOLDEN
"Where the west remains," which we changed in the '70s to
"Where the west lives," a prophetic declaration to the future.

He'd say, "If a place makes you feel that good about being
there, aren't you going to come back? Aren't you going to stay
longer? Aren't you going to tell your friends about it so they can
come too?"

I don't know if Golden realizes it, but it's been given a great
distinction above all other places. Besides being a gateway to
the Rockies, it has been given the honor of being the "Seat of
Western Hospitality."

So my question for you is this:
What's your sign?
Does it speak well to those who don't know you?
Or does it reject them?
What attitude does it project towards strangers and
passers-by?
Do people feel welcome around you
or do you push them away?
So show me,
what's your sign?
As it is written:
"Do not neglect to show hospitality to strangers, for by this
some have entertained angels without knowing it" (Hebrews
13:2).

P.s. For all of you that are reading this, if you ever happen upon our quaint little town, from my grandfather to me, and now from me to you, I'd like you to know that "You Are Welcome."

Eagles High

I had climbed up the rockslide, carefully navigating the huge boulders so as not to fall or hurt myself. It is always a bit exhilarating and makes for a wonderful workout, like doing cross-fit. The mountain silence was filled with peace. And the warmth of the afternoon sun caressed my face. I heard an eagle call off in the distance, his cry echoing up the ravine. Looking to find the source, I scanned the sky above me; nothing. So I looked out towards the horizon; nothing. Hum, where is he? Something caught my eye high in the sky as I rescanned the horizon. There they are. There were two of them, high above the horizon, circling, watching for the next meal. But this was unique. They were so high I could hardly see them. Actually, I have never seen them this high above the ground. Yes, I have seen them quite high before, but nothing like this. As I was marveling at the fact that they could still see their prey that far away, the Lord spoke to me clearly, but in an inaudible voice that resonated inside me. He said, "They were outside of their box. Even though it was higher than usual, they could still operate just as efficiently as if they were lower. They could see more, though, incredibly more."

They were so far out of range that nothing would ever see them coming. Actually, nothing could ever see what they saw either, and so effortlessly at that. Stretching the limits, going outside the known boundaries, new frontiers. Everything is possible, for, with God, nothing is impossible; new horizons that couldn't be seen until they flew higher are now clear; things that weren't attainable before now are. They were so high now that I couldn't even see them until I climbed higher. The more I climbed, the more I saw, just like them.

We are being called higher, you and me. We didn't even think we could see from there, but we can. Actually more. We will see a bigger picture without losing any detail. More strength is required, but it's a strength we already carry; we just don't realize it. From this new level, many things are actually easier. And there is the kind of wisdom that only comes with seasoning. So consider yourself well-seasoned. The new level is not like the others. It's not new levels, new devils. No, not at all. But rather, it's new levels, new power, new authority, new wisdom.

I think you should stretch your wings a little more
and see where you end up.
It's an invitation from the Lord.
I'm going to.
I'll see you there.
I look forward to it.
In the wild blue yonder.
Yep, life is good.

Racoon on the Roof

Around 2:30 in the morning, Michelle woke me up from a deep sleep and said, "Hear that? It's something big, and it's walking on the roof!" I listened, and sure enough, there was something walking on the roof, and it was definitely bigger than the squirrels we regularly hear, a lot bigger. Then we hear the sound of wood being chewed and ripped out of the roof, and I wonder if this is real or if I'm dreaming. Sitting up, Michelle says, very perplexed and bothered, "I think whatever it is, it's ripping a hole in the roof; listen to that." I had to agree that's what it sounded like, we could actually hear the wood being ripped out and shredded right above our bed, and I realized, *Hmmm, I'm not dreaming*. I also realize that if I don't do something now, that thing is going to end up right in our bedroom. Just what we needed was some mystery animal destroying our roof and terrorizing us in our own home. So I sit up on the bed and put my feet in my shoes and walk through the door from our room onto the deck outside. All the while, I'm thinking to myself, *What do I have to confront now, and what the heck is big enough to actually rip out the roof?*

It's really dark tonight. There's no moon, and it's cloudy, so I can barely see the outline of our roof. I stood still and listened;

no sound but the softly falling rain. Back downstairs, I rummage in the dark closet feeling around for my big mag light. I didn't want to turn the house light on because my son Garrett and his friend had flown in for the weekend and were sleeping on air mattresses on the living room floor. Then out of the darkness, I hear, "Dad!" What are you doing?"

"Well, Garrett, something big is on the roof, and it sounds like it's tearing it up. So I'm trying to find my flashlight, so I can go see what it is."

Back upstairs and out back, I shine the light slowly across the roof while listening intently for any tell tail sound; nothing. I go down the stairs under the tree just outside the kitchen window. Peering up through the branches, I carefully search for any sign of a big wood shredding animal. Again, nothing. Stepping out from under the tree to go around to the front, I feel the cool, soft rain on my head and shoulders. Thinking through the sleepy haze in my brain, I realize that all I have on are my shorts and that my untied shoes are flopping around with every step, and heck, it's a little cold out here in this night rain.

As I'm contemplating what if I have to run in shoes that will fly off of my feet, a movement catches my eye on the dark mass of the roof, and immediately, my focus is off of me and back on my mission. Shining the light in that direction, I see it, a large raccoon, at least thirty-five to forty pounds, crouching down, hiding next to the dormer; his eyes shining brightly like little lights right back at me in a sinister sort of way. "So you're the wood shredding culprit." I was surprised to find out it was a raccoon. Before I can even think, I find myself shouting at the top of my voice, commanding him, "Off my roof in the name of

Jesus." He immediately jumps up and disappears over the top to the other side. *Well*, I thought to myself, *that worked pretty good.*

The front door bursts open, and out flies Garrett, "Dad, Dad, what's going on?"

"It's a raccoon! And get my flannel shirt hanging with the coats by the door." I know, after the fact, I should have said coat for the rain, but I didn't. I'm still coming up out of the fog of a deep sleep.

Now we head to the back, looking intently for the culprit. No raccoon. Back under the tree by the house. No raccoon up there in the branches. Back out front where I first saw him. No raccoon. Slowly scanning the rest of the roof by the other dormer. *There he is!*

His beady eyes were shining again in the light beam. I can't let him get away with this, and I have to be careful; raccoons can really be nasty. I know because of many past experiences with them.

Once my friend Brian was searching a person's garage to see if one was there and if we needed to trap it. As Brian walked by a shelf on the wall, something screamed a blood-curdling scream and landed right on top of his head. It kept screaming like a wild banshee while it scratched furiously at Brian's eyes with its claws. It was crying out with an unnerving, unearthly scream, and Brian was yelling loudly in pain and shock as he bounced wildly back and forth off the car then off the wall like a pinball. In total shock at what was happening, he was slapping furiously to dislodge the thing from his head. He finally was able to get a handful of fur and grab the thing off of his head and throw it down against the floor. His cheeks below his glasses and his forehead above them were ripped open with gnarly scrapes and gashes; blood covered his face and was dripping swiftly off his chin. If Brian hadn't been wearing glasses, the raccoon would have scratched his eyes out.

Another time we were called to trap one that had ripped the head off of a family's small bulldog and left it by their back door like it was leaving them a grisly present. So no, this one is not getting away, so it can come back later. I'm not taking any chances, and it's not ripping through the roof into our bedroom. I have no choice; I have to act now! I have to protect my home and my family.

By now, Michelle has all the lights on in the house and is finishing putting her shoes on downstairs. "Get my gun!" I yell emphatically as she opens the front door. She steps across the pretending to sleep friend of Garrett's, grabs my shotgun off the hearth, jumps back across him, and brings it out to me. You see, Garrett's friend is a city boy who knows nothing about country living, nothing about guns, and nothing about wild animals except what he's seen in cartoons. He finally sat up and asked what was going on! Michelle told him we were after a wood shredding raccoon, and he immediately laid back down and pretended not to hear and to be asleep. But this character is another story.

Handing the flashlight to Garrett, I raise the shotgun to shoot. "Keep the light on him, buddy; I need to see clearly to get this shot." He's facing us, and his head is only six inches from that upstairs window. If I don't do this right, not only will I blow a hole in the roof, I'll break the window, too. No pressure here. I position myself, so when I shoot the shots at the same angle as the roof, so I don't destroy our house, and I point slightly more to the left than you would for a direct shot, so I hopefully don't blow out the window. I pull the trigger. *Kaboom!* The blast shatters the quiet of the night and echoes off the mountain behind us. Then plop. The pest slides across the grass in front of us and settles at Garrett's feet. No more huge holes in our roof from pesky overgrown rodents, thank God. It was a perfect shot, no damage to the house. It was actually a miraculously good shot; in the dark at that, I know I had some unseen angelic help.

Looking back near the dormer where we first saw the pest, there's a mangled wad of insulation the size of a basketball laying on the roof that had been pulled out of the hole he already chewed, and shredded wood is strewn everywhere. He really was ripping the roof out right down to our bedroom. Raccoons can sure be destructive. "Great!" I say out loud, "At least I stopped him before he could do any more damage." Just what I wanted was some animal to make a large hole in the roof while it's raining, and of course, it's directly over our bed.

The same raccoon had also ripped a three-foot hole in the roof of our shed a couple of days earlier. He savagely destroyed many things inside. It was like he was carrying out a vendetta; he was exceptionally destructive.

As I pondered this situation, the Lord used it to show me that sometimes we wait to confront something because we don't think it's as bad as it really is. The whole reason for a confrontation should be to solve a problem and its fear that usually keeps us from doing so. Sometimes we simply need to hit it head-on and remove the threat before it destroys something that is important or is even a threat to our well-being. Just like this raccoon tonight.

As Christians, one way we confront things would be by our prayers and the scriptures we speak out that we are standing on because there is such great power in the Word. The Word is our weapon against evil and problems alike. When we speak the Word, the Holy Spirit does amazing things. Sometimes the consequences for us not taking action are devastating. Just like this raccoon tonight, if I hadn't taken care of the problem now, it would have quickly escalated and gotten much worse. I had no choice; I had to act now! Can you imagine what would have happened if he had gotten into the house? Our home is our sanctuary; there are some things that just don't belong there.

Jesus' confrontation with the money changers in the temple was violent, but the temple was cleansed. Whenever He cast out demons, it was violent, but the people were set free. When He spoke to the fig tree, it was intense, but He showed the power of words. When He spoke to Peter and said, "Satan get behind me," it was humiliating but showed the truth about the source; it was Satan and not Peter. When He called the Pharisees snakes, it caused a violent reaction because of their pride and hardness of heart, and it showed the people the truth about them. He confronted the problem of no food with a wonderful miracle and fed thousands. He confronted the problem of a wedding party being culturally shamed by turning water into wine.

May all of your confrontations accomplish much, go smoothly and solve problems. May you be led by wisdom and leave things better than they were before in Jesus' name.

It is written the kingdom of heaven suffers violence, and the violent take it by force. That would be us. That would be Christians expanding and protecting the kingdom.

Sometimes we need to take a stand against injustice,
sometimes we need to confront evil.
As the old saying goes:
"The only way for the triumph of evil
is for good men to do nothing."

Babies in Heaven

Michelle sat quietly, rocking so very slowly, staring blankly out the sliding glass doors, tears occasionally welling up then streaming down her face; she was so lost in a sea of sadness and anguish. She had just miscarried our baby, and the guilt that it was her fault was more than she could bear. The pain would build in waves, and she would sob uncontrollably, then it would leave, and she would get some relief before it would build again.

At first, we had been speaking that a baby so soon in our marriage was not a good thing. Michelle felt she had made a mistake. She was wishing she wasn't pregnant. We had talked about it and had decided that we really didn't want a baby right now.

Then we visited my brother and his family in Wyoming. We chased some coyotes that had been stalking and killing the calves, bumping and bouncing in the pickup across a vast open pasture. Then we bumped along to another pasture and checked on some other cows and calves to make sure they too were doing well.

After we got home, Michelle started spotting blood. She was cramping for about a week, and then she lost the baby. In hindsight, we couldn't believe we went bumping around in a truck knowing that she was pregnant. We felt so irresponsible. But you know, sometimes when you're in the midst of things, you don't always make the best decisions. Sometimes you don't realize what's happening until it's too late. That's where you wish you had used some wisdom, some common sense. She wasn't showing yet, and she wasn't feeling bad, so no one knew she was pregnant. Even Michelle didn't realize that maybe she shouldn't be doing that, riding in a bouncy pickup, until the end of the day, when we got back to the house. She wasn't used to being pregnant yet and protecting that little life inside of her.

At a point where her grief was feeling unbearable again, the glass doors became like a cloud that came out of nowhere, and all of a sudden, there was Jesus in front of her draped in a well-fitting white robe, snuggled safely in his big strong arms was a little, bald, newborn baby. Behind him, the angels were singing and dancing and rejoicing all around. Confetti was floating down. It was very happy and festive. She could see everything except Jesus's face. So she asked him, "What is this? What am I seeing?"

He answered, "This is your baby born into heaven. Like all miscarried or aborted children, they are born into heaven. We celebrate every birth into heaven. This child is happy you have chosen life in Me, and it will be waiting for you when it is your time to come."

In the conversation, even though Jesus didn't say it, Michelle was shown that the power of our negative words had brought about everything that led to the miscarriage. Our words and our actions, alike.

Proverbs 18:20-21
"With the fruit of a man's mouth his stomach will be satisfied;
He will be satisfied with the product of his lips.

Death and Life are in the Power of the Tongue,
And those who love it will eat its fruit."

What a hard, painful lesson about our words. Ouch!

Michelle was so thankful the Lord showed her where the children are that have been lost. The comfort and the peace it gave her was overwhelming and brought such joy, such healing to her hurting, broken heart.

She then asked Jesus to forgive her, which He very graciously did. He didn't rebuke her, and He didn't condemn her. Then He had Michelle forgive herself. When she did, all the guilt and shame and pain disappeared. Jesus loved her, and even in our sins, He still loved us. He didn't agree with the sin or condone it, but He still loved us. What an incredible God we serve!

Just as quickly as the vision appeared, it disappeared, and Michelle was again looking out at the pasture and the mountains behind us. This time in peace, now forgiven, now free, now she can move on with her life. Thank You, Jesus! Only a couple of times in her life has Michelle had such a vivid vision.

Since we've been married, Michelle has had a couple of miscarriages, and before I knew her, she had an abortion. The doctor and a family member convinced her that it was only a mass of cells, nothing more. But immediately afterward, lying in pain both physically and emotionally, all alone on the cold metal table in that dark room, she knew they were wrong; they had lied to her. She felt so betrayed by them and foolish that she had believed them. When Jesus forgave her, and she forgave herself, it also included this. The betrayal, the shame, the guilt, the anger and hatred and torment she felt about the whole situation ever since that day all left. It just disappeared. The tearing in her heart that came from the abortion was healed, and she felt whole again. He totally redeemed her from this tragedy. Also, Michelle felt that the miscarriages were judgement on her because of the abortion, but Jesus let her know that was not true. He doesn't kill babies. He creates them; He heals them—what a relief from a wrong belief.

In Matthew 8, Jesus healed the leper because He was moved with compassion. His grace, His goodness He offers to us because He loves us. When we are in Jesus (by simply being born again), whatever does not measure up to the glory of God disappears, and His grace covers it all. He generously offers undeserved forgiveness, undeserved love, a love that cannot be earned, and undeserved favor. He will redeem us from the deepest pit. No matter how we got there because, like the leper, He has compassion on us.

"Jesus Christ is the same yesterday, today and forever" (Hebrews 13:8).

Jesus met Michelle where she was today, reached into her past, and healed it, creating the way for her to go into her future totally free, totally healed, totally whole.

"The Spirit of the Lord God is upon me, Because the Lord has anointed me to proclaim good news to the poor; He has sent me to bind up the brokenhearted, To proclaim freedom for the captives And release from darkness for the prisoners" (Isaiah 61:1, NIV).

"The Lord is near to the brokenhearted and saves those who are crushed in spirit" (Psalm 34:18).

Jesus gave Michelle beauty for the ashes of her life, the oil of joy for her broken heart, which healed it and also healed her womb. Now the tears streaming down her face are tears of joy because she knows how much she has been forgiven and how much He loves her.

We both look forward to seeing our children that are in heaven waiting for us. One has her name; the other is waiting for his. Like us, if you have children waiting for you in heaven, then you will see them when you get there. And they will love you. Yes, they will love you.

As David said in 2 Samuel 12:23, speaking of a child that had died and that he shall see him in heaven. "Can I bring him back again? I shall go to him, but he will not return to me."

The purpose for women is to create life, and what a glorious and honorable purpose that is.

The sadness of this action, this loss of life, is something that inspires Michelle to this day to encourage unmarried mothers to keep an unwanted pregnancy and use the gift that God gave women of giving life.

When you *know the pain*, it's easy to help others not to go there.

The Flood

We rejoiced with a great celebration the first day we could get a car up to our house. It took over eight weeks to make the road passable again. The road between our home and the bottom of the meadow had holes the water had torn out that were over four feet deep; the channels where the water dug beside the road were over three feet deep. Rocks the size of basketballs and smaller littered the places the water had flowed. And the road itself? Impassable, totally destroyed. It had been the bottom of a raging river, and it definitely looked like it.

As the rain began to fall, the Lord told me, by way of a simple but extremely strong impression, to take the car and park it down the mountain around the corner. So I did. Boy, am I glad I obeyed. Otherwise, we would have been stuck for weeks, with no way in and no way out. The way it looked at the beginning was pleasant. A soft falling rain and the dry brook where the spring runoff gently flows were bubbling happily with water. It was peaceful; it was beautiful. We awoke the next morning to another world; sheets of rain were falling hard, blowing sidewards in the wind, and the pleasant little brook had become a raging torrent, we could hear it roaring along half a mile away, and it stayed that way for almost four weeks. The road was no longer a road, but a seething, turbulent river, flooding down our mountain road.

So we would walk down to the car through the rain, the raging water, and the obstacle course it had made. We had to take dry clothes with us to change into once we got to work. Then after work or doing our errands, we would walk back up to our house. It's a half-mile each way, and it's a good thing we had the hay meadow to walk through because that was the only way to get to the house. Even the meadow had water flowing through it for days. At first, it was almost a foot deep. Then as the water receded, it got down to ankle-deep, then just a trickle.

The hardest part was walking up or down in the dark after work; sometimes we had flashlights, sometimes we didn't. Getting home late at night and navigating the holes, all the separate rivers of rushing water, the mud, the rocks, and the pouring rain without tripping and falling was a little difficult. For Michelle, the hardest part was not letting fear take over. At night with all the noises and all the animals around, it can be an incredible torment in your mind. That's where you really find out what you're made of, what you really believe, and whether God is really with you or not. I must say the peace of God showed up every time. And you know, once you control your mindset and your beliefs about what is true and what isn't true, then life is much happier, and the walk back and forth in the black of night isn't nearly as hard.

At the beginning of the storm, once we saw how devastating and difficult the situation was becoming and the hardships we would have to endure, we had to make a decision not to let what was happening around us and to us steal our hope. We decided together to have a "we can handle this, and we're going to make it through to the other side no matter what attitude." When we did that with determination, it became not just our hope but our belief, and it made it many times easier to navigate through the hardships that had come upon us. We clung to the expectant belief that the Lord was guarding, guiding, and providing along the way, which He did in marvelous and usually subtle ways. We also spent a lot of time meditating on and speaking out Scripture verses having to do with protection, provision, and deliverance, which kept us from falling into despair.

You'd think that because you're high on a mountain that you are at least immune to floods. Heck, we're over 1,000 feet above the nearest flood plain.

Not so. You think your roads and way of life will always be there, you know, at least be mostly the same, that things even in hard times won't change that much. Not so. You find out quickly how much you believe in the Lord and how much faith you have in the things of this world. Your phones don't work; your power is off for who knows how long, which means no light or heat. You have to use candles or gas lamps, no stove to cook your food on, the wood from the woodshed is floating in a pond, and your refrigerator doesn't work. Your money is worthless because it has no value here in this situation, and if you need some, there is no way to get it anyway. And are you an important person with important titles? No one cares; they are meaningless now. Your money, your prestige, and your titles have no power to keep destruction away from you or help anyone else for that matter.

I stood on the deck behind our house, watching in amazement as water was flowing down the mountainside everywhere I looked. Waterfalls were crashing over every one of the 10,000 plus rocks. The whole mountain had become one huge, massive stream. It was truly astounding. There was not one place where water was not either flowing or pooling and then only to cascade further down the hill. The sound of so much moving water was almost like thunder. I thought to myself, *This must have been what it was like at the beginning of Noah's flood.*

"Like the sound of many waters, like the sound of loud thunder" (Revelation 14:2).

Looking down under the deck, I noticed all the water from the hillside directly behind us was flowing up against the back of our house. So I hurried downstairs to see what was happening. When I first saw how much water was coming through our back window into our living room, I thought, *Oh no, we're in trouble, big trouble.* And I fervently prayed, "Oh, Lord, our house is built upon You, You are our rock, so I thank You that our home and we will be saved. You said You would be with us in trouble and that You would deliver us, thank You that You do it *now*. I now command the water to go around our home and not in it in Jesus' name." I said this over and over with great urgency for quite a while until it felt like something had been accomplished, and I didn't need to say it anymore.

John 14:13-14
"And whatever you ask in My name, that will I
Do, that the Father may be glorified in the Son.
If you ask Me anything in My name, I will do it."

Night had fallen, and after about half an hour, the water quit flowing through the window and down the wall. We were so incredibly relieved. Once morning came, we went outside to look behind the house to see what had happened; how had this prayer been answered? The water was parting before it reached our back wall and flowing miraculously around us on all sides. Our house was spared.

(Whoever heard of a house high on a mountain spared from a flood? What a miracle!)

The parable about building your house on "the Rock" is a bit more real to me now. Everything is destroyed but you, and you get to watch it happen all around you. The importance of a spiritual rock underlying all of life is magnified, especially when you know that everything can change in a day. Praying in the Spirit comes in pretty handy at times like this. We did it a lot. Your true beliefs are revealed, then tested, then stretched beyond what you think you can handle. You know, the thing that made the biggest difference for us was when the rain started, and nothing appeared even slightly wrong, and I obeyed that still small voice, anyway, and moved the car down the mountain out of the way of what would become the floodwaters. Even though we had to walk a mile round trip, it gave us the access to the outside world that we desperately needed.

Times like this are good for reassessing what's important and what isn't, what should be changed and what doesn't need to be, what boxes do we have parts of our life in that need to be removed, who are your friends and who aren't, and what do we do with our life from here?

Yes, we were forced to miss work and lost out on a lot of income which was hard on us, actually very hard; somehow, though, God made it work even though the numbers didn't add up. But aside from all of that, I sure got some interesting pictures.

The flood deceptively began with a beautiful, softly falling rain.

Dog Attack on Red Dirt Hill

We were living on Red Dirt Hill, a spot between Winter Park and Granby in the Colorado mountains. The fall weather was so absolutely beautiful Michelle decided to get the wagon for baby Travis and take a walk down the dirt road in front of our house. She lovingly laid a blanket down in such a way that he could sit up and hold on to the sides as they went off on their little adventure.

The fall flowers, the butterflies, the warm sunshine, birds singing and flitting happily between trees, the clean, fresh smell of the mountains was all so invigorating. Especially to be able to walk in it and share it with our first child. She felt like she was in some sort of paradise as she shared simple sights and things with the happy wide-eyed baby.

They had ventured along for a while when for no real reason, she happened to look back up the road she had just come down. First one dog, then another and another and another and another darting back and forth mischievously across the road as they trotted in her direction. They were quite a ways away but coming closer quickly. Something felt wrong about them, actually more than wrong; it felt bad, even dangerous. They all had a wild look about them, and as soon as they noticed Michelle and the baby in the wagon, they started to run straight for them, barking as they came.

Immediately Michelle knew she was in trouble, so she frantically tried to pull the wagon and run. Realizing she was getting nowhere real fast, she stopped, turned, grabbed baby Travis out of the wagon just in time, and held him close to her. The dogs weren't just wild; they were vicious and stopped just before reaching her, then began snarling menacingly as they slowly circled around, very methodically, with their ears back, their shoulders hunched, and the hair raised straight up on their backs like they do as they size up their prey just before they attack.

Somehow Michelle knew they were after the baby, so dropping his blanket in the dirt, she pushed him as high above her head as she possibly could, her heart beating out of her chest as thoughts of what to do next frantically raced through her mind.

She couldn't run; she couldn't even move, much less walk to get away as the pack of dogs had surrounded her, sized her up, then started jumping in the air barking ferociously, snapping and snarling, as they tried to bite and rip Travis away from her. She was so focused on protecting her baby that she could feel the sheer terror of the situation, but it never came upon her; it never affected her, she was willing to die to keep him safe, and she felt like this was it. Like she was going to die. But that incredible mother's instinct, that powerful determination to protect your children no matter the cost, kept her standing strong. It's something you don't think about; it's something you just do.

Suddenly in her mind, the only thoughts were Jesus, Jesus. So she screamed it out with all her might. Jesus, Jesus, Jesus, Jesus, Jesus, Jesus, Jesus. The dogs quit jumping at the baby; they calmed down and started sniffing around at the ground like they had found an attractive scent to follow. Wow!

Incredibly relieved but not sure she was safe yet, she continued to hold our little buddy high above her head. In all of this, the baby amazingly never uttered a sound. Then a neighbor up the road came outside and called one of the dogs. "Oh, you bad boy, leave the people alone, come on, come to Mommy, oh good boy, Mommy loves you!" It disgusted Michelle to watch as he ran to his owner, wagging his tail the whole way like nothing had happened at all. That broke things, and the pack disbanded, and they all took off, each going their own way. And the owner? She was in denial that anything bad could have happened at all, especially by her dog.

An interesting thing is that the dogs never tried to attack Michelle; they only wanted the baby. She never got bitten, just bumped and hit, but not harmed. Also, once the name of Jesus was spoken, everything changed; the danger was stopped, the terror was removed immediately. All of the dog's behavior changed. By the power, in the name of Jesus, my precious little family was totally and completely delivered in an instant.

The Unimaginable Choice

Base camp was right at the DMZ, the "Demilitarized Zone," the line that separated North and South Vietnam, which of course, the enemy never honored, but then when does the enemy ever honor any agreements we make with them. The devil is not bound by our honor, so why are we surprised. The men were all resting awhile from never-ending missions into the jungle and were milling around like they were on their favorite street corner with their friends. American jets were flying low overhead because they'd been called in to deliver Americans from certain death by the Viet Cong. You could hear the combat in the distance. An occasional mortar would come flying in, usually just disrupting things and never hitting a viable target (thank God), throwing dirt in the air and reminding everyone that they were still in a war. The guns were clean; the socks were not; circumstances have a way of changing priorities.

He was resting in the shade just inside the gate, just watching the other men walking around talking of home and telling jokes they probably wouldn't tell their mothers. His eyes would alternate between them, the road out the gate and the jungle.

The enemy was watching them; he could feel it stronger today; they were always watching from hiding places just out of sight in the jungle nearby. It was an eerie feeling; actually, it became unnerving if you thought about it too much, but it reminded you of where you were and not to forget to be ready, to always be ready because they could attack at any time, you may have to stand up and fight at any time.

Just then, a helicopter landed on the outskirts of camp, probably bringing in fresh supplies. His mind went back to how his platoon had arrived here. They were moving fast, right above the treetops, when machine-gun fire riddled the side, shattering the glass, piercing holes so shafts of sunlight shown in. There wasn't any more room in the back, so he was sitting in the co-pilot seat up-front with the pilot, who turned with a sly grin saying, "It's scary at first, but you get used to it." The man looked out over the jungle below, trying to see where the gunfire was coming from when another blast scoured the side again. He felt something wet splatter his face and something plop into his lap. Looking down, he sees it's the pilot's brain, he's covered in blood, and no one is flying the helicopter. He doesn't remember anything after that; all he knows is somehow, by some miracle, he had flown the chopper himself and landed safely right in the middle of camp. He always believed in his heart that an angel helped him that day and saved all their lives.

The movement of people a few hundred yards away crossing the road going back and forth from their villages to the fields brought him out of his memories and back to the present. You never knew if they were the enemy or not because the enemy looked just like them. Suddenly, like out of nowhere, he noticed a little girl appeared from the field and was walking towards the open gate. Like any two or three-year-old, she stumbled when she walked but kept on coming forward. It was odd, though, such a little person and no one nearby, no adult with her at all, and she just kept walking towards the gate.

He could feel something was wrong, but he couldn't tell what, so he just kept his eye on the little one as she stumbled and bumbled her way towards the gate. The guards noticed her too and watched with amusement as she continued on. Just then, the breeze picked up and lifted her skirt up over her head. *What! Is that what I think it is? Surely it can't be. Surely no parent would do that to their precious daughter,* he thought to himself. Again, the breeze lifted her skirt up over her head, and again, he saw it. A band of explosives tied around her. His mind was reeling with jumbled thoughts. *What should I do? How could someone do this to their baby? Oh, my God, she's getting close enough to blow up twenty or thirty unsuspecting men; oh no, the guards didn't see it; they don't know, she's still walking towards the open gate. What do I do? What do I do?* Quickly he brought his mind back into focus. *Okay, if I run out there, they will blow me up when they blow her up. Same thing if I run and jump on top of her, I can't save her because they are watching, and they'll set off the explosives, though, that would save the other men. Oh my God, it doesn't matter what I do; the little girl will still die.*

Oh my God, how can someone do this to a child?

Still agonizing with his decision, he brought his gun up, aimed, and pulled the trigger. The little girl fell to the ground. *Oh, thank God,* he thought to himself. *At least she didn't suffer.*

Looking behind them to see where the shot came from, the guards saw him motion to them to be careful and waited to hear what he had to say. He ran up to them, motioning wildly with his arms and explaining what he saw and what just happened. All the people watching from the field ran for cover in the forest. They were watching to see how many Americans were killed. Not one was harmed. They all knew exactly what was really happening. The soldiers moved carefully to within a safe distance of the bomb still wrapped around the little girl and then froze. Not because of fear, but everyone was still trying to wrap their minds around the idea that the enemy, the North Vietnamese, would actually willingly kill one of their own precious children in order to kill Americans. The idea was so unthinkable to the American mindset it was actually beyond comprehension.

While they stood there waiting for a bomb tech to come upfront to help figure out what to do next, the enemy in the forest shadows detonated the bomb. Silence and incredible sadness fell upon the Americans as they moved back through the gate, each pondering how ruthless, brutal, and heartless the enemy they were fighting really was.

Now years later, rocking back and forth on the couch in agony, his head in his hands and tears streaming into puddles on the floor, he was saying, "How can God forgive me? How can He ever forgive me? I didn't want to do it, but I couldn't let all those men die. The pain is still with me; will it ever heal? Did I do the right thing? Did I make the right decision? Is there any way to right the wrong done to that little girl?"

What can you say to that? I sat in silence for a few moments. I didn't know what to say, so I asked God, "Okay, Father, what do I do now? What do I say to him?" Immediately the words welled up from within me. "Tell him I love him." So I told him God loved him.

"How?" he cried out. "How can he love me after what I have done? I don't deserve His love."

"Now what?" I said out loud to the Lord, and the words came up again, "Tell him the girl was going to die no matter what he did, and his choice though painfully difficult was to save his men, which he did, and many are still alive now with families and productive lives and many children of their own." The Lord continued to give me more words, "You had an unimaginable and incredibly difficult choice to make, and you had only a few seconds in which to make it; no matter what you chose, her people had already chosen to kill her, so she would have died no matter what you decided. There was nothing you could have done to save her."

"Had you done nothing, many of your friends would have died that day, and you would be lamenting your decision more to do nothing and let them die than you would the decision you made to save their lives. There are literally a few hundred people alive today because of your choice. And to help you feel better, the little girl is with Me, she never felt any pain, and she's happily here in heaven waiting to see you and tell you that she loves you too."

"What! How can that be?" he cried, the tears dripping off of his chin as he looked at me in unbelief.

"Let's ask God to forgive you, then just repent in your own words. Now you also need to forgive yourself."

His face so contorted with the agony in his heart was released, and a peace fell upon him; he was basking in a love he'd never known or even heard of before, the Holy Spirit was touching him deep in his wounded heart in ways I'll never know, healing things, deep things and wounds and scars that needed to be healed.

In a few moments, right before my eyes, the face of the man beside me changed; it wasn't the same face; he didn't even look like the same man. The hardness that the pain of his life had caused wasn't there anymore. It was gone. The guilt he'd carried for so long was gone; he was free. Free for the first time he could remember. It was pretty incredible to witness it right before my eyes.

I know there are other vets out there who can relate to this story.

Before you judge his choice, remember this man had only seconds to make an unimaginably difficult decision. And that no matter what he decided, someone was going to die.

I never saw this man again. We just never know what these chance meetings the Lord arranges for us will accomplish. I suppose that's why He tells us in the Bible to "make the most of every opportunity" (Colossians 4:5).

May the Lord help us all to hear His voice and make the best decisions possible no matter what the circumstances may be in Jesus's name.

Difficult Decisions

There are decisions that we sometimes must make
that are prickly and difficult, beyond what we think
we can handle, but the Lord will seal our hearts and
minds with His peace and promises to give us that
flower of wisdom when we need it, even in the midst
of the pain, and the strength to do what we must do,
if we will just ask.

(James 1:5, and Philippians 4:6-7,13)

Flipped the Car

It was New Year's Eve. We were spending it with a group of friends, enjoying each other's company, listening to good music, singing, worshiping, praying in the Spirit, and intermittently praying for each of us and the country for the upcoming year. And there were lots of good things to eat and drink. We made a long night of it on purpose. Everyone was off the next day; all the kids were taken care of, so why not.

Getting home later, around 1:30 a.m., we discovered Garrett wasn't there yet. He should've been here long ago, and now we were worried. He was always home on time. Why was he so late? Where could he be? No message on our phone.

Garrett was working at Evergreen Lake as one of the skate guards. Great job, lots of other teenagers especially cute girls. He loved it. He was sixteen, and it was after midnight. One of them that he had wanted to date and knew from school needed a ride home. How convenient. Well, almost, she lived miles away on a ranch back in the woods. But heck, he liked her, so why not. How far? Who cares! He was with the girl he wanted to be with, and that was all that mattered. Taking his time which they both enjoyed, he slowly took her home. A goodnight kiss and a promise for a date, and he was headed off home on cloud nine.

The driveway was about five miles long, winding through the woods to a beautiful old log homestead. Pressing on the accelerator, he sped along the old dirt road, still thinking about that girl when...*boom...smack...crack...crash*. He'd taken a curve too quickly and lost control and was headed really fast straight for a tree. "Oh Lord," he prayed, "don't let me hit that tree," just as he prayed that the car flipped and rolled a number of times until it came to a stop without hitting the tree.

Finding himself on his side, he hears the music blaring and reaches to turn it off. His hand hurts, and it was bleeding. He could move his arms and legs, but he couldn't get out of the car; the door wouldn't open. He hears steam blowing out somewhere, something dripping, and a ticking that sounded like the car was going to blow up. Then he realized the car was on its side, that was why the door wouldn't open, so he kicked out the other window and climbed out, totally disoriented and in shock, and started to run.

The only thing on his mind was to get away from the car before it exploded and get to the safety of the girl's house and call us. He ran and ran and, after going on for a long way down the dark forested road, he stopped to get his bearings. He realized he had no clue where he was or the way back to the girl's house. His light jacket wasn't enough for the cold winter night. He could feel himself weakening because of the trauma of the wreck and the frigid Rocky Mountain night. It felt like all of his energy was slowly flowing out of him. So he turned and ran for a long time in another direction he thought would take him back to the house. Stopping after a while to look around, he realized there was still no house, no lights, nothing familiar.

He had the painful realization that he still didn't know where he was.

He's starting to feel confused. He didn't know it at this point, but his thinking had been clouded by the shock from the trauma of the accident. He was completely disoriented, and easy decisions were all of a sudden not so easy. It was a short walk back to the house from here, but he was so bewildered he chose the wrong direction.

Strange sounds were coming from the dark forest on both sides. The sound of hoot owls and the howls of nighttime predators were coming randomly out of the woods. He was starting to feel afraid. He still had no clue where he was, and in his mind, it seemed like some animal was going to come out of the dark and attack him. The only light was from the moon. The shadows all around began to look menacing; the dark forest on both sides of the road began to feel evil. Suddenly he hears animals running nearby; it sounds like a whole herd of them pounding the ground, snorting loudly, and breathing hard; all he can see are glimpses of odd moving shapes in the moonlight before they disappear again into the darkness. He couldn't tell what they were or if they were going to attack him, so he froze in his tracks, not sure what was happening. Not sure what to do. Then as quickly as they started running, they disappeared. No sound now; all is quiet again except the occasional hoots and howls off in the forest.

The battle in his mind for control of his thoughts had become intense. As he continued to walk to keep from freezing and maybe find a way out of this mess, his imaginations filled with all kinds of fear began to bombard his mind like a sledge-hammer. Then he began to hear, "It's so hard for you; why don't you just lay in the ditch until morning." He would say, "No!" but the thoughts just kept pounding. He knew it wasn't the Lord, and he also knew that if he did lie in the ditch, he would be dead by morning. So he just kept saying no to the fearful thoughts and pressed on in the hope and belief that God would help him and he would be rescued.

Walking towards a light that seemed to have just appeared out of nowhere in the distance, his hope jumped within him. *I'm safe; I'll be able to get help*, he thought. He was so relieved that he sprinted up the mountain in that direction. Turned out it was only guarding an old abandoned mine. As he approached and realized no one was there, his hope began to drain away.

Fear was coming out of the darkness at him. He was cold and beginning to feel desperate. Now, what to do? As he wondered about that, a song welled up from within him, and he began walking and singing..."My God is an awesome God; He reigns from heaven above in wisdom, power, and love, my God is an awesome God," over and over. He would sing for a while then start saying loudly over and over, "God is with me, and I will make it, God is with me, and I will make it in Jesus' name." Then he would start singing again. He said the fear lifted off of him and the night sounds weren't scary anymore, though he still didn't know where he was. The battle over the thoughts and imaginations in his mind stopped. What an incredible relief that was. So he stretched out his arms and prayed with great fervor, "Father, I need help; I need someone to come to rescue me because I don't know what else to do, and I don't know where I am. Jesus, help me."

He kept walking to ward off the piercing cold, and the moonlit road with all the strange, moving shadows continued on for what seemed like an eternity to him when suddenly a pair of headlights bathed him in their light. As the car cautiously pulled up, he began begging, "Help me, please help me."

The kind lady said later that she knew something was wrong before she even heard his pleas for help. "No one ever walks on this road at night, especially this far from any of the few homes up there," she commented. She noticed that he also didn't seem threatening to her, so she felt safe stopping for him. Once he was in her car, she could tell he was hurting and in shock. Getting ahold of us somewhere around 3 a.m., she explained where she would be parked and waiting for us to pick Garrett up. I spoke quickly to him to discern how he really was, then we hopped in the car and sped almost an hour to the meeting place. I was glad he was not hurt badly, but I could tell he was still in shock and emotionally drained from the whole ordeal. He had been wandering and struggling with fear and cold and hopelessness for hours.

The kind lady explained everything well as we hugged and loved on our son, thankful he was okay. She seemed like an angel to us even though we knew she wasn't. (Or was she?) Driving up the road to find the wrecked car, we were stunned to see the condition it was in. It was lying upside down and sidewards in the road. The roof was smashed clear down into the headrest, and the outside looked like it had been pounded in a shower of boulders. Shattered glass and various pieces of the car were strewn all over the road. Somehow God miraculously helped Garrett survive without being crushed. He only had one cut on his hand and a bunch of bumps and scrapes.

Realizing we needed to clear the road so folks could get by, we went to the ranch house, and the girl's parents graciously offered to help. I had Garrett sit in the van and watch as we hooked up the car. He was shaking from the cold and the trauma and so thankful to have been rescued. Michelle stayed in the van to comfort him and watch him and talk to him, making sure everything was okay and to determine if we needed to take him to the hospital or not. Turned out we didn't need to. As the shock wore off and he began to warm up, the clarity of his mind returned. The gracious cowboy and I had to yank the car back onto its wheels, then he towed it back to the house with his pickup, with me doing my best to lay sidewards across the seats and steer the mashed wheels forward to keep it from going off the road, which didn't work very well, so we just drug it kind of sidewards most of the way.

Were we mad at Garrett? No. We understood. All would have been well if he had made better decisions, especially the driving part. We didn't have to discipline him. He learned many things that fateful night that he carries with him to this day. One thing was that when you are all alone, and there is nothing and no one to help you, even when all seems lost, that God hears you when you cry out to Him using His Word and will not only help you but deliver you too.

I also know that all our prayers that night helped to keep him from being hurt badly during all the parts of the whole ordeal. Plus, all the hours we spent praying for our children and teaching them how to pray by example paid off well because he practiced what we taught, and it helped save him. Thank You, Jesus. God's grace was huge that night!

So much for telling your teenager not to go anywhere after work and come right home. Were any of you reading this ever teenagers?

This is the scripture he uses for the lessons he learned that night:

> Rejoice in the Lord always; again, I will say, rejoice! Let your gentle spirit be known to all men. The Lord is near. Be anxious for nothing, but in everything by prayer and supplication with thanksgiving let your requests be made known to God. And the peace of God, which surpasses all comprehension, will guard your hearts and your minds in Christ Jesus.
>
> Philippians 4:4-7 (NKJV)

Seven More Demons

Several Christian bands joined to play in a park in Manitou Springs on a beautiful Saturday for a concert. The idea was to attract people with the music and then pray for anyone who had a need of any kind. People began sitting around on the grass, enjoying the music, playing frisbee, people watching.

On a bench nearby Dixie, Michelle's mom, noticed an odd-looking woman sitting by herself, dressed in very dark colors with amulets around her neck. She approached her, started a conversation, and the woman opened right up, saying how much she needed prayer. So, Dixie called Michelle over, and as they began to pray, the woman cried out adamantly, "Don't touch me, don't touch me!" She put her hands up and leaned back as far away from them as she could. Michelle and Dixie gave each other a quick glance of wonder not because of what she said but because of the way she said it, in an angry sort of way. It took them off guard; they'd never had that experience before when they had prayed for folks. So they stepped back and gave her some more room and said they would be happy to pray without touching her. You know, sometimes, as Christians, we get in a rut thinking that a certain way of praying for people is the only way to pray. But it's not! The Bible is full of many different and varied ways of doing it.

After praying according to her request, Dixie asked her to come to our church sometime and gave her our phone number. The lady had said how much she has problems with demons and nightmares and that she wanted to talk to someone who could help her with them. That week she called Michelle and wanted to know more about our pastor and if he could help her, and how did she know that he casts demons out. Is he able to cast all of them out, and once he does, are they able to come back? Good and interesting questions from someone who wasn't a Christian, someone who wouldn't normally even know to ask such things. Michelle explained how we had witnessed a number of people as they had demons cast out of them and that some would scream, some would writhe on the floor, some were just very angry, and others shook uncontrollably. Then the demon came out, and the people were visibly different and had a peace and relief and clarity they hadn't had before. Most of the time, if there was more than one, they all came out, sometimes all at once, sometimes one at a time. And as far as them being able to come back, well, we would discuss that with her if and when any are cast out.

She wanted to come to church only if the pastor would cast out the demons. She didn't want to know anything about Jesus; she didn't want to hear anything about Jesus. "Just cast out the demons, and I'll be on my way" was her attitude. Something was obviously not right about that, but we couldn't figure out what it was. We really didn't think she was going to come, but sure enough, she showed up and sat with us in the pew. She wore a black dress, kept her sunglasses on, and had her hair, so it partially covered her face like she was trying to hide. She looked very peculiar, would only look down at the floor, and refused to speak or even acknowledge anyone except a few words to Michelle. As soon as praise and worship began, she started moving her head back and forth, moaning and rocking in her seat. We still didn't know much about casting demons out of people but had seen enough to know that the demons in her were not happy. They were starting to manifest through her. She looked absolutely miserable. Before service, Michelle had pointed her out to the pastor, so he spoke with her and said that he could help set her free. She had said that's what she wanted.

After the music, he had everyone turn and raise their hands towards her, and she got so frightened she cried out loudly, "No, no." He comforted her and told her she didn't have to be afraid here and had everyone put their hands down and turn around towards the front; then he had the music start up again, only softly this time. Coming to her, she allowed him to put his hands on her head, and he prayed quietly and commanded the demons to leave and loose her. Her posture immediately changed and relaxed, and a smile came for the first time to her face. You could actually see the peace that had fallen upon her. It was like she had transformed from ugly to attractive right before our eyes. She was happy and spoke freely with us and actually hugged us and then left saying she would be in touch.

Michelle spoke to her that week, and the lady said there were demons stuck on her window outside her home wanting to come in. Michelle said to rebuke them in the name of Jesus and seal her home with the blood of Jesus. She adamantly refused to do it; she said she didn't want to get rid of them. Then she said something very strange, that she wanted them there, she actually wanted them. Like she was even going to invite them in. Even though she tried, Michelle was never able to speak with her again; her voice was always garbled, and when she did speak, it was unintelligible. The pastor also tried to call her a few times to follow up but had the same results.

Something was very wrong with this whole thing. As we put the puzzle pieces together, it just got stranger. We couldn't figure out what it was. Finally, one day as I was praying in the Spirit, the Lord showed me a picture of her. I saw it in the form of something like a vision, but I was also aware of the things going on around me at the same time. I saw that she was a practicing witch, and she was stronger than she had ever been before, and she was enjoying her newfound power. But she was more tormented than before. She was using it to control, manipulate and intimidate and hurt people. I thought to myself as I watched, *Surely this can't be true, and then on the other hand, if it is, then why did we not see it before?* She wouldn't accept Jesus as Lord and Savior and then protect herself with the blood of Jesus because she wanted the demons; she wanted them back inside possessing her. She was hesitating at first because she liked the peace her freedom gave her, but then her lust for power grew stronger, and she chose that and the demons instead. Wow! I would never have figured that out if the Lord hadn't shown it to me. I had no clue that people would actually do this. Then I saw a scripture; it was this one:

Now when the unclean spirit goes out of a man, it passes through waterless places, seeking rest, and does not find it. Then it says, "I will return to my house from which I came"; and when it comes, it finds it unoccupied, swept, and put in order. Then it goes and takes along with it seven other spirits more wicked than itself, and they go in and live there; and the last state of that man becomes worse than the first. That is the way it will also be with this evil generation.

Matthew 12:43-45

So, I wondered why she would go through all that trouble, and as I was thinking the Lord showed me that once the original demons were gone, they came back just like the scripture said, with seven more wicked and powerful than the first one was. Then I understood. We cast the demons out, and others more powerful than them come and possess her, and now she is seven times more powerful than she was. Wow, that's terrible. The torment that comes with all the other demons has to be incredibly miserable. Who would think of such a thing? A witch that wanted more power was the answer I got. Hmmm...but the price they pay for more demonic power is paid in fear and torment and pain and eventually their own destruction.

I told this to Michelle but no one else because I didn't think anyone would believe me. Then one day, we ran across a man who used to be a pastor that, when he realized he wasn't called to be a pastor, stepped down and began a counseling and deliverance type of ministry because that was where his heart was. The way he was talking, I knew he would at least understand what I saw. So I told him. He said, "Oh yea, that same thing happened to me about five or six times before I finally caught on. The same group of three witches would show up about once a month at church, I would cast the demons out, and they would leave totally delivered. Then they would come back all possessed and want me to cast the demons out again. Once I caught on, I realized I was helping them get more wicked and more powerful every time because of the scriptural promise that seven more would come back and occupy the empty house. So, I bound Satan over them and commanded them to leave and never come back in Jesus' name, and I never saw them again."

That was the answer to our questions. Since then, we have found others who have had similar experiences. It's nice to know we weren't the only ones ever duped by this ploy. We were being used in a demonic plot and had no idea what was really going on. Now we do, and we aren't fooled by that stuff anymore. I've read it somewhere that we learn more from our mistakes than anything else. Well, in this instance, we sure learned many things that we will never forget. My grandmother used to say if it doesn't smell right, then don't eat it. If something about the situation doesn't smell right, then we don't do anything anymore until we know why and then what to do.

After being duped because of our lack of knowledge and understanding, we determined not to let that happen again and began to study about how to improve these things and our discernment. We found out that, for one, it can come by practice and training. But solid food is for the mature, who, because of practice, have their senses trained to discern between good and evil (Hebrews 5:14). It comes from wisdom, from the Scriptures, from the Word; it also can be a gift from the Lord. So we began to practice a lot, to read the Word a lot in places that were helping us and giving us insight at that particular time, and to ask the Lord for the anointing to discern more accurately and those gifts from 1 Corinthians 12, especially the word of wisdom, the word of knowledge and discerning of spirits.

Have we arrived and always get it right? Nope. But we are definitely better at it than we were before. You know, one thing that has helped more than anything else is simply asking the Lord what to do, listening for His answer, and then doing whatever He said. And another thing we learned from these experiences was that casting out demons was a whole lot easier than we thought. It's all in the power in the name of Jesus, not us.

That was a problem I had at first, thinking it was my power, or my righteousness, or my holiness that helped make things happen. Until the Lord made it clear that it was His power, His righteousness, that I received because of Jesus, and the power in His name that made anything happen. Once I understood that it was easy to speak the Word and then watch Him perform it. It took all the pressure off of me. I didn't have to try to make anything happen. He made it happen; He worked the healings; His power made the demons leave. He sure has a lot of grace for all of us, even in our foolishness and ignorance.

"Heal the sick, raise the dead, cleanse the lepers, cast out demons; freely you received, freely give" (Matthew 10:8).

"What is this message? For with authority and power He commands the unclean spirits, and they come out" (Luke 4:36).

But the Helper, the Holy Spirit, whom the Father will send in My name, He will teach you all things, and again...But when He, the Spirit of truth, comes, He will guide you into all the truth, and again...The words that I say to you I do not speak on My own initiative, but the Father abiding in Me, He does the works.

John 14:10,26;16:13 (NKJV)

The Avalanche Almost Got Us

Coming down Berthoud pass towards Denver just past the last switchback, Michelle looks up the side of the mountain and says, "Wow, look at that, the snow is moving, it just burst like an explosion into the air from the peak, it looks like the whole side of the mountain is sliding down, it's an avalanche. It's amazing; let's stop and watch it." I stopped and looked way up the mountain somewhere above timberline and could see the snow coming. I wanted to sit and watch it too, but had this overwhelming urge to move farther down the road to see it better. It was a feeling like an urgency so great that I couldn't help but go. Michelle was saying stop, stop, stop, but all I could feel was go, go, go. So I moved the car a little further down the road. Within seconds the avalanche had not only made it to the bottom of the mountain but crashed into the deep ravine between it and the road, shooting up the embankment about seventy yards then furiously surging across the highway eight feet deep right behind our car. Michelle saw all this happen out of her window. I was watching in the rear-view mirror; one moment, the road is clear, the next, the avalanche had bulldozed its way across it. I could hardly believe what I had just witnessed. It happened so quickly; it took it just thirty seconds to come all the way down the mountain, up the ravine, and cross the road, and then it was over.

If I hadn't moved forward that little bit, we would have been overcome by all that snow-filled with dirt and debris. It missed us by only thirty feet! Just thirty feet! It could have killed us! Totally astonished, we got out to look at the now silent avalanche on what was left of the road; that's when we got to see the rocks that were half the size of our car caught up in the snow and all the trees that were ripped out of the ground and snapped into hundreds of pieces. You just have no clue about the immense power in an avalanche until you see the devastation it causes up close and personal. The pass was closed for the rest of the day so the road crew could clear it out. The cars right behind us would have to go back to Winter Park and all the way around through Kremmling, an extra two to three hours, or spend a long night waiting.

I realized after the fact that the overwhelming feeling in my gut to move was the Holy Spirit impressing on me to get out of the way, to get out of the way now! Like "twist my arm; get out of the way now" kind of a deal!

You know, He speaks to us in so many different ways, each one appropriate for each of us and unique for our specific situations. Lots of times, we're obeying and don't even realize it was Him speaking. Of course, this time wasn't even a voice, just a "whop me upside the head with incredible urgency to move" feeling and the idea of getting a better vantage point. Heck, I didn't realize it was the Lord until after we got over the exhilaration of just being missed by a killer avalanche and were well on our way down the road. Just looking at those cute little baby faces strapped in the back seat made me realize the gravity of an almost bad decision and how their lives totally depend on my choices no matter the outcome. It made me want to hear the Lord better.

It's amazing how some life and death decisions don't feel important until you've made them and then seen the results after the fact, either good or bad. For this one, I only had seconds to decide and didn't even know it. Makes you want to hear the Lord more clearly and make better decisions, doesn't it?

God and Disaster

You know, power outages and natural disasters like massive storms or floods or avalanches or earthquakes are so unsettling and can be very destructive, but they happen. Aside from doing whatever is wise for preparation, I have found that my best protection is to pray scriptures of protection over my family, our lives, and our homes and property. Of course, there are challenges, and I haven't always seen the answers that I wanted, but I have seen amazing miracles of deliverance by doing so.

"Unless the Lord guards the city, the watchman keeps awake in vain" (Psalm 127:1).

May the Word Be Planted

May His Word be planted in your hearts.
His kingdom planted in your lives.
May His wisdom be planted in your tongues.
His vision planted in your eyes.
May His power be planted in your deeds
and may all that you do be blessed.

The Skier

We were sitting in the front row at church. Which actually wasn't that hard because this church was small and only had two rows. It was in Fraser in an old wooden building right on the road going through town. Our Pastor JR Polhemus had a guy up-front that had obviously just come off of the ski hill at Winter Park. He was a jolly-looking guy; his hair was pasted against his head in some places and sticking straight up in others, he had rings around his eyes where his goggles had been, and he still had his ski pants on that squeaked when he moved. He said he'd been driving by and saw us here and had a strong urge to come in.

Before he even let the guy sit down, JR pulls him up-front and says, "Well would you like to know Jesus, would you like to be born again, would you like your sins forgiven?"

With a big grin, his teeth shining out through his beard, the guy says, "Sure." After leading him in a short prayer, we could all see that God had touched him. His face was gleaming like light was coming out of him.

Then JR says, "Would you like to be baptized in the Holy Spirit? It's another wonderful gift the Lord has for you; would you like everything the Lord has to give you?"

"Sure, but I don't have to get wet, do I?"

"Nope, you don't."

"Well, okay, then."

So JR lays his hands on him and simply says, "Be baptized in the Holy Ghost in Jesus' name." The guy's eyes shot wide open, and he looked like a bolt of lightning went through him, and he immediately began praying in the Spirit, the words flowing out of his mouth, tears streaming down his face as he lifted his hands to heaven. It really impacted everyone in the room. We could all feel a strong presence of the Lord, and there was this heavy blanket of incredible peace upon the whole place.

Michelle looks at me and says, "Well, if he can do it that easy, so can I," and she closed her eyes, asked the Lord to help her, and began praying in tongues like she'd been doing it all of her life. It came out so easily. I was shocked. An overwhelming joy came over her while she sobbed and kept praying and praising God. I figured, *Well, if they can get it that easy, then so can I.* So, I closed my eyes and prayed for God to help me too, and it was like I could feel these words in my chest and throat. Words I had never seen or heard before came, so I just said them, and as I did, they seemed to float out of my mouth. I didn't have to try to make them up; they simply came to me as I spoke them. First, I could feel them, then I could see them, then I spoke them. Michelle said that for her, she could see the words in her head, and she just said what she saw. And they just flowed out from her.

We never saw the skier again, never knew his name. But up till then, I'd never seen anyone touched by the Lord like that guy was. It was fun to watch it all happen right before our eyes. And

Pastor JR? Well, he was Mr. Happy all night long, praying for people and watching God touch them and speaking wonderful things over everybody. It was truly an incredible service.

These are the three scriptures we use now to help folks get baptized in the Holy Spirit and pray in tongues; it works all the time. We just say them, and God works in the people.

Luke 11:10-13

Acts 2:4

Romans 8:26-28

From the Grip of Death to Life

We had been at this for hours; she still hadn't dilated very far, and I was having a hard time keeping my eyes open. So, Michelle suggested I lay in the other bed in the room, and I quickly fell asleep. Michelle's contractions had gotten consistent enough and close enough that the doctor had said to come on into the small mountain hospital. So here we were.

Actually, she had been having contractions for two days before they started getting close enough together for us to come to the hospital. Once there, the nurses suggested we walk up and down the hallways because it would help get the process going. The hospital was so small we probably walked the whole thing at least one hundred times until the contractions got so painful Michelle couldn't walk anymore. We asked for something for the pain and to help her relax, but the nurse informed us that this is a catholic hospital, and they don't believe in giving you any drugs. We tried to explain that the pain was becoming unbearable and that with the first child, once she could relax, he came out fairly quickly after that. But the nurse wouldn't listen, and the doctor wasn't there yet.

Awaking an hour or two later, I see she is still having contractions and having to breathe through them to control the pain. So I ask her how she's doing, and with one of those "you've got to be kidding" looks, she rolls her eyes and continues the special breathing. Michelle had said that she didn't think the baby was going to come for a while and, "Go ahead and rest," so I laid down again in the bed next to her and went back to sleep. It's amazing how well you sleep in an uncomfortable situation when you're tired.

Soon I awoke with a start. I shot straight up in the bed, my eyes still trying to focus. I could feel this incredible urgency in my heart, and so I asked, "What's going on?" Still great travail and pain but no baby, Michelle was struggling, actually really struggling hard and not doing well at all, and this had been going on for way too long. If she wasn't in such terrible travail, she would have been crying. For some reason, they had been monitoring Michelle but not the baby. The nurse finally checks the baby and almost goes into a panic as she calls the doctor. It was around 4 a.m. by now, and he had decided to rest until he was needed again.

Now the doctor is in the room checking her, the baby inside, and the monitors. He looks very distraught and, with great urgency, begins yelling for the nurses and fiddling with all the tubes and cords. "Get her ready for a C-section," he says. "The baby isn't going to make it if we don't get it out now! Every time there are contractions, its oxygen is cut off, and it isn't getting any air; something is wrong." Then he commanded the nurse to give her some kind of shot for pain which gave her a little immediate relief. He was your typical small-town country doctor with a big heart and had been on the phone line for quite some time with some other doctors down in Denver, and the more they talked, the more bothered he got. Not a very good sign.

He became so concerned it was obvious he thought the baby was already dying; he just was trying not to show it to us. Michelle had been fighting so hard and so long that there was a lot of concern about her now too. They were also wondering if she was going to make it. The situation had suddenly become very grave. The nurses rushed frantically in a controlled sort of way, making preparations, their faces dull with a fear they were trying hard not to show because I was standing right there watching.

I had to control my thoughts and not let death and disaster in my mind because it was right there; we could all feel it; it was heavy in the room. I tried to focus on the few scriptures I knew and believed that God would help us. So out of desperation, I just started praying in the Spirit. I had finally gotten baptized in the Holy Spirit only a couple of months earlier (thank you, Pastor JR Polhemus). Silently at first, but when I realized they thought the baby really was dying, I let it loose. I mean with all the intensity and passion I felt in my heart. "My little baby is not going to die! Neither is my wife!" I stood there speaking to Michelle and the baby inside, I thought I was doing it in a low, quiet voice so no one could hear me, but Michelle said it was so loud that it was echoing throughout the whole hospital. Oh well!

I quickly got so single-minded and intently focused that I wasn't aware of anything else around me. It was like I had entered a realm with just me and God, and I wasn't stopping until

I had a good result, period! The nurses were gently pushing me to different places around the room to keep me out of the way as they worked. As I prayed, I was determined that the baby would come out naturally with no C-section and that my little one would live and be sound and whole. I also didn't want Michelle to be cut up if she didn't have to, and neither did she. I could feel power, God's power, as I prayed. I knew the Lord was moving, I could sense it, I could feel it, it was on me and in me and heavy upon us all. You could tell it had replaced the death and disaster.

Sure enough, after a little while, right at the moment, they were getting ready to roll the bed into surgery. Michelle says, "I need to push."

The doctor yells out, "Nurse, it's coming; get me some gloves! Nurse! Gloves! Gloves!" Then with great exasperation, he says, "Oh never mind, here it comes." He got his hands in place just as the baby shot out. I mean, like he was shot out of a cannon. Ka blueeee. Doc caught him like you would catch a football.

And there he was, a precious son, a little warrior that never gave up even to the point of death, bright blue from the lack of oxygen with the umbilical cord wrapped tightly around his neck. Because of the trauma from almost dying as he was being, born his face was squished with anguish and pain. He looked like Yoda from the movie *Star Wars*.

The doctor was a Jew, and the way things transpired was miraculous. God was speaking to him in a way he would understand, through a medical miracle. He just stood and shook his head a lot, mumbling to himself, his eyes wide with wonder at what he'd just witnessed. I thank God for the good doctor and the wonderful, caring nurses; we wouldn't have made it without them, and I thank the Living God and His power to heal, deliver and perform miracles.

Thank You, Jesus, for delivering
my wife and my son
in many more ways than one.

Oh, one more thing.

I think the hardest part of the whole ordeal for Michelle came eight days later when Doc had us come in for the circumcision.

Doc lays him on this high table, turns to Michelle, and says, "Here, hold his legs for me." It wasn't so much what he had to do that got her; it was the blood-curdling scream of pain and shock from our tiny little buddy that put her over the edge. It pierced her heart. It took her a while to get over the trauma from that event.

She occasionally talks about it to this day.

This is Travis on top of Indian Head.

Balancing Act
A difficult place to be,
when life feels like a balancing act
prayer is the safety net
that you can't see.
Things that seem impossible become easy
once you know how to do them.
"For nothing will be impossible with God."
(Luke 1:37)

Three Pairs of Golden Eagles

Michelle answered the door to find Wagner, our landlord, standing on the porch. We were living on ninety-two acres on the side of a mountain, in a 160-year-old house built of hand-carved stone that looked out over Denver. The view was incredible, day or night. Wagner and the Mrs. lived about 200 yards away in a home he had built when they retired about twenty-five years earlier. At the back of the house, there was a thirty-foot high, meandering waterfall and pools that flowed into a fishpond with a stone Japanese-type bridge across one corner of it. Koi rested peacefully among the waterlilies.

When they had moved in, a landscaping friend gave him a dump truck full of iris bulbs. There were literally thousands of them, which he planted in artistic arrangements across the whole ninety-two acres, along with poppies and all kinds of wildflowers, ivy, all kinds of non-native cactus, and various ground covers. They were even on outcroppings of the cliffs around the hay meadows that got mowed three times each summer. Water from the original spring and any runoff were channeled into five strategically placed ponds across the big meadow in front of our house. Besides the chokecherry and wild plum that grew profusely all over, he had planted about one hundred fruit trees; Crabapple, two kinds of cherry, pear, apricot, peach, three kinds of plums, chestnut, and about eight different kinds of apple. It was a veritable botanic paradise.

His vegetable garden, one of the joys of his life, just steps from our house, was a series of terraces accentuated by the well-constructed stone retaining walls that kept them in place. If it could be grown in this climate, it was in his garden, which he shared abundantly with us.

And animals? If it's from Colorado, we saw it at one time or another in our place. We even saw red, brown, silver, and black foxes. A black one lived near our house, and we saw him regularly for about three seasons. He was a playful joy to watch, especially in the snow, where he stood out like a sore thumb. The owls would answer my calls as they spoke to each other at night. Michelle could get the crows, and especially the turkeys, to answer her.

After we had lived there for about five years, Wagner had come by to tell us we had thirty days to find another place and move because a grandson and his wife and child were going to move in. At the same time, I had some extremely difficult dealings with a publisher who wasn't doing anything they were supposed to. It was incredibly frustrating. No, it was maddening.

When I found out about Wagner's decision, which was so unexpected that it shocked us, he told us often how much he loved that we were living there. It couldn't have come at a worse time. I realized then that all the issues coming against us were too big for us, so I decided to fast. No food, just water with lemon for at least three days and more if I needed to. The Lord had miraculously provided this beautiful and peaceful home for us to enjoy, and it was not time for us to leave.

I continued with my work writing and took long breaks to pray in the Spirit and speak Scriptures over our situation. I would say, "No, it's not time for us to move, and our lives will not be disrupted." Because anytime there is such confusion, torment, and frustration, there is usually something else involved. Then I would speak this from Psalm 91:14-16 over and over again:

"Because he has loved Me,
I will save him;
I will set him *securely* on high,
because he has known My name.

He will call upon Me, and I will answer him;
I will be with him in trouble.
I will rescue him and honor him.

I will satisfy him with a long life,
And show him My salvation."

I had to read it! I had to speak it! I had to pray! For us, the situation was destructive, and we desperately needed God to intervene and deliver us.

Michelle had begun frantically looking for somewhere to move, even though at the time, we had no extra money and couldn't afford rent somewhere else. Prices had sky-rocketed because of the recent cannabis invasion. It would have forced us to be homeless until we could figure something else out. She didn't know what else to do, and she couldn't sit idly by while things were so desperate.

I told her the next day after I had started fasting that we were not going to move, no one was going to force us out, and our God would deliver us. Some way, somehow. And that she didn't need to look elsewhere for someplace for us to move to. She was skeptical, didn't know as she really believed it, but hoped it was true.

The second day of fasting was even more intense. The pressure against us was almost unbearable. So I simply prayed more throughout the day and with more passion.

The third day was beyond unbearable. The bleak thought of being forced out and being destitute, of being homeless, was miserably hopeless. I turned my desperation to passion in my prayers and began yelling them out, even screaming them out; otherwise, hopelessness would begin to take over. And it felt like we would die.

In the afternoon of the third day, on the back deck facing the cliff, as I was crying out for God to move, to deliver us now, I felt something break in a spiritual way. As I look up, a golden eagle is diving from high above the cliff towards me. I watched in awe as he passed, lightning-fast only a few feet away between the trees; he was even with my head, only about ten feet above the ground. I could hear him whooshing by.

They never do that!

I knew it was a sign for me that God was answering my prayers. I looked up towards the cliff again, and here came a second eagle, same trajectory, same lightning-fast speed. But this time, it called out as it sped towards me, the cry echoing across the mountain.

Unbelievable!

Then it happened again and again. Six times and six golden eagles flew by, confirming to me that not only had God heard my prayers but that He was going to answer them mightily. And it wasn't just six separate golden eagles; it was three mated pairs.

Truly astounding!

Truly amazing!

Truly miraculous!

I'd never seen or even heard of anything like this before.

Wow, what an answer to prayer!

Not just an answer for today,

but also for things in the future.

I mean, *wow*!

It gave me the peace I needed.

God is good!

So what happened?

Two weeks later, Wagner came to tell us he had good news, that things had changed, and we didn't have to move, and that he was happy it turned out that way. (Praise God!)

It took an excruciatingly painful two weeks, up almost to the day we had to get ready to move before the sign of the eagles came to pass. Yes, we had the miraculous sign. Yes, we now had hope, but it's not complete until it comes to pass. I still had to continue to press in with the prayers until something happened. Because, again; It's not complete until it comes to pass!

Michelle kept looking around for alternatives. But the more she looked, the more hopeless she became. She was moving in her own strength, her own plan, not what the Lord had told us or His direction, and things were only getting worse. She realized she was being driven by fear. So she prayed:

"I believe Lord, but help my unbelief, *help* my unbelief."

It was miserable; it was agonizing every day that we had to keep waiting, keep hoping, keep standing on certain scriptures, and say them over and over.

"Faith is the substance of things hoped for, the evidence of things not seen" (Hebrews 11:1, KJV).

We were reminded how both Joseph and David had to go through thirteen distressful and traumatic years before their promises came to pass. That's a long time! The promise is always there and is always true. It's just that between the promise and its fulfillment, sometimes we must go through fire and not give up.

It was not easy standing like we had to. Michelle and I were finally so relieved that we weren't going to be displaced and that we would stay until it truly was time to leave and not before. Amen!

Now that God had finally delivered us.

It was time to celebrate!

And the publishing issue? They finally finished my project, not well, but just barely okay, then they spiraled out of business. Sadly, they were unprofessional and underhanded with me.

Taking a stand using the Word with the power of prayer and fasting is wonderful. Wonderful because of the results. Though definitely not easy. It's a decision, to begin with, then a journey that we must walk out.

So, what did the sign mean?

A number of things.

It is layered with meaning for me.

The biggest takeaway is that He loves me and cares greatly for me.

Then, it meant that God was going to move concerning our home and living situation.

And next, that He would turn around my publishing situation. Which didn't happen like I thought it should, but it was resolved enough to move forward.

And again.

The six eagles are six full years I have to wait for something. The three mated pairs are multiples of double portions that will come to me. Six in this instance speaks to me of a convergence between heaven and earth. It speaks of a divine reset, a divine reversal, a supernatural intervention, all in a specific season which is to come. It is also much bigger than me. This was also a strong confirmation to me that He will surely bring the current situations and future things to pass better than I had hoped for or could imagine. We are excitedly waiting and expecting these good and miraculous things to come to pass.

Many times, God speaks to me to confirm things with eagles and with fire. Though, the interpretation can change with the circumstances. He speaks to people in many different ways. I suppose the hardest thing for all of us is to know whether it's really Him communicating with us or not. That's why, for me, I sometimes need some kind of confirmation. And many times, that confirmation is peace.

The Standoff

It was one of those incredibly beautiful Colorado summer days where it's hard to stay inside and work. So Michelle steps out onto the front porch to enjoy the day when she hears footsteps nearby and turns and sees a herd of deer browsing around on the hillside next to our house. Everything was calm and peaceful until one of the big does walks within about twenty yards of Michelle, stomps her front foot strongly into the ground, and lets out a long, loud snort. Michelle looks right at her and says, "You goofy deer, are you challenging me?" The doe points her ears forward, stiffens her neck, and stomps her foot again, but this time, the loud snort was like a trumpet. And she's doing it right at Michelle. She's challenging her and trying to intimidate her. This happened about three times.

She was stunned. *This doe is really challenging me at my own house in my own yard, no less. That darn deer means business. This is crazy! Since when do deer come and challenge you on your own front porch?* So Michelle speaks to her and says, "There's no threat here. Now you stop that!" The doe stomped her foot down hard again and did her snort/trumpet challenge again. So what do I do? Michelle thought. *I'm not retreating from a silly deer.* She heard the Holy Spirit say to just act like you're eating. So she pretended she was eating an apple and smacked loudly. The doe stopped and stared at Michelle for a moment, then bent down and began eating contentedly at the tall grass. No more threat. The challenge is over. Amazing. The Lord has an answer for everything in life.

I Didn't Know I
Wasn't a Christian

I had just finished a strong discussion with Michelle's brother-in-law; we were kind of dating at the time. You know, still going out with other people because it wasn't a serious relationship, besides I figured until I'm committed to someone, I'll do what I want, and she felt the same. Anyway, he told me that if I didn't have Jesus that God wouldn't hear my prayers, besides all the sin stuff. So, I thought about it over the next couple of months. Michelle had gotten born again a number of years before under Billy Graham's ministry. He spoke a truth to her heart she had never heard before, and it changed her life. She loves that man and looks up to him like a daughter looks up to a good father.

I grew up in the "we believe in healing, but Jesus was a good man and a prophet, but He is not Lord" group. For instance, once I broke my wrist, and it was miraculously healed, and throughout my life, I'd had numerous other things healed also. Some of them instantaneous, others over a short period of time. So did my dad, as well as cancer in his lungs. We had seen and experienced so many healings that when we came across

Christians that said healing wasn't for today, I just thought they were stupid, and I didn't want anything to do with their dead, unbelieving religion. My family and many others I knew were being healed today, so how could anyone in their right mind say that healing wasn't for today? It just didn't make any sense to me.

I knew God was real; I talked to Him all the time, and many times, I could hear Him. I believed in the Holy Spirit; I just didn't believe that Jesus was the Messiah and that salvation came through Him. I didn't understand why we needed to be saved. The way I was taught, there is no hell; we thought it was a false belief. I also could see spirits, hear spirits and feel them when they were nearby. But all the so-called Christians that I had ever met said such things weren't true or even possible. Some believed there were angels and demons, but none believed that we could see them or know when they were around. So because of that, I stayed a long way away from any main line religion church folks in America. No one believed in the things I experienced and saw on a regular basis, so I wanted nothing to do with them. Also, the religion I grew up in doesn't believe in evil spirits. They say it's just wrong thinking. Well, I'd seen and experienced demons with my own eyes, so I knew these guys didn't know what they were talking about either. But at least they believed that God heals today.

Scientologists got ahold of me for about two weeks in college. That is until I figured out their beliefs were a bunch of malarky, and they wanted you to pay all your money to hear them. I don't think so.

Then I got this great job. I was one of the first divers at a place called Casa Bonita, a restaurant in Denver with a huge waterfall and pool, caverns, plazas, and tropical forests all filled with strategically placed tables people could eat at. After a month or so, there were about eight of us, and we all knew each other from our competitive diving when we were younger; some of us had even been on the same team.

We were required to dive once every two minutes until they figured out that was too much and changed it to once every three minutes. They wanted twenty dives an hour. Ole Bob, the diver manager, would be out there hiding behind a rock or a palm tree timing us, but we would always see him. His leg, his arm, or a part of his head was always sticking out from behind his hiding place.

We dove from a height of about twenty feet, next to the waterfall, into a tropical pool below that was fourteen feet deep. The little wood plank we stood on to dive from was just big enough for our feet. After diving into the pool, we'd go under the waterfall and through a short underwater tunnel back to the hidden diver's room, dry off, warm up under the heat lamp a little, and climb up the ladder to do it again.

Then ole Bob told us he was changing our jobs a little, we were going to have to play the villain Black Bart, jump onto the stage (next to the diving platform) from eight feet up the cliff to surprise everyone, have a short dialogue and do a gunfight with the sheriff over a damsel in distress and end up doing a controlled fall into the water. Then dress up in a gorilla suit, jump around the nearby tables like a gorilla, and steal a pre-placed purse from some lady nearby in the audience while being chased by the animal trainer, then bungee jump in the gorilla suit, almost smacking the water with your feet and pop back up onto the stage and scare everybody that had been chasing us. Thing was that darn mask always twisted sideways when we grabbed the bungee vine and jumped, so we couldn't see where we were going. We had to feel where we were as we were moving through the air, then pop back and "kip" at just the right moment onto the platform on the cliff. Now that took a little getting used to because you didn't really have a second chance to get it right.

Next, we were going to have to wear a leopard skin, Tarzan outfit held together with Velcro, and juggle fire torches in the dark with lightning flashes and rousing jungle drums beating for a couple of minutes, then finish by diving into the pool to put out the fire. So the idea was a different show every fifteen minutes, all while keeping up the dives in between. Then it starts over again every hour. "And guys," ole Bob says, "you have two weeks to get it all down, or you're fired."

Black Bart and the Gorilla Act were easy, but none of us could juggle, much less torches in the dark. But it's amazing how quickly you pick it up with a little motivation and practice for about one minute between every single dive for two straight weeks. We all had little bruises all over our bodies from head to toe, where we'd hit ourselves practicing with the torches. And the first time with live fire was exciting, to say the least. Nobody had any hair left on their hands or up their arms. A few eyebrows were missing too. For our first live show, it was a bit disconcerting to find out that the fire from the torches is your only light, then trying to juggle without dropping them with the rain, the lightning, and the jungle drums beating wildly. But we did it. Everyone got really good at it. We had to train ourselves to see certain clues in the dark to show us where the handles of the torches were and to learn to do it by feel.

The most fun with fire dives, though, were the doubles. The second guy would dive into the pool and scale the cliff on the other side of the waterfall. Then the first guy would throw the lighted torches one at a time. Second guy would reach out and catch them out of the air, then both of us would juggle till the drums ended, then dive into the pool at the same time. We would occasionally miss and have to retrieve the still-burning torch from the plate it was stuck in at the table behind us. You should have seen the look on those people's faces when that happened. Priceless!

One of the guys was Mike, a very strong ex-wrestler who could dive and came from somewhere back east. He was the first Christian I'd ever met that knew that you could be healed today and that spirits, both good and bad, were real and that some people could not only sense them but see them as well. I marveled that I had actually met a Christian who believed in these things. We had great discussions dressed as Black Bart with our six guns, or Tarzan with our burning torches, about spirits and healing and spiritual things.

At this point, I still believed I was a Christian though he knew I wasn't. I mean, I was in a mainline religion, so that makes me a Christian, right? And besides, if you're an American and believe in God, that makes you a Christian, right? But he was always kind and understanding; he never condemned me. Every time he took a break, the other employees, the servers and bussers and such, would throng around him and sit with him at the table. People loved him, and he loved people, and they knew it. He was just a wise and good guy who didn't judge anyone and, because of it, brought many to Christ. I saw it happen over and over again.

This was the first place that I saw that you didn't have to be some preacher or be in the ministry to fulfill your calling. I always resented that people said and believed that being in the ministry was a higher calling. If that were true, then that meant that nothing any of the rest of us do is worthwhile or even important, and I knew that just wasn't true. Where would the preachers be without someone to build their homes, make their cars, unclog their toilets, grow their food, or bury their dead? I realized that no matter what job you have that God will use you there because that's probably where you're called to be and what you're called to do at the time, which would mean that that is our ministry. That's what God did for me by having Mike there to talk to while we dove. I believe those folks get "more important and higher calling" mixed up with simply esteeming and honoring those in the ministry like it says in 1 Thessalonians 5:13.

One of my grandmothers always coerced us to come down and go to vacation Bible school. We came down to see them and our cousins and play out on the vast ranch they had. We just put up with their boring Bible school to do that. Besides, all the adults were old, strict, not really that nice, and had bad breath. Why would anyone want to go to a church like that?

One time when we got down there, Grandma's right eye was bright bloody red. She looked like she'd been kicked in the face by one of the horses. "So, is that what happened, Grandma?" I teased.

"No, son, no," she said, all flustered. "I was singing at church with all my might, and I popped a blood vessel in my eye."

"You what!" We were dumbfounded. How could somebody do that?

"Yea," she responded. "The doctor said to quit trying to sing so hard." Then I got it, I remembered. You see, all the older folk, especially the old women, would sing as hard and loud as they possibly could. I can just see their eyeballs popping out and bouncing across the floor. Can you imagine hearing a song where all the loud, off-key old women are trying to outdo each other? It was a sight and a sound to behold, I assure you. I don't know where God was in that church, but they assured me He was there somewhere. And He probably was; I just couldn't tell. They definitely didn't believe that God heals today even though He had healed me, and they didn't ever have a good answer about demons and the spirits I knew were around, so I never brought it up. It caused unnecessary arguments with the people I loved.

As I grew and became a teenager and into my 20s, I realized I really didn't like people who called themselves Christians. There were actually some groups of them that I hated. They were incredible hypocrites, condemning my friends and me as sinners, then going out and doing similar things themselves. They were also the most hateful, judgmental, unforgiving, critical, ugly, gossiping, unhealthy people I knew.

They were also easy to pick out. The men were harsh, the young men were wimps, the women were ugly, and God's love was sadly missing. When they would say I could get born again and be like them, I would cringe; who would want to be like them? When they said I could be forgiven of my sins and join them in heaven, I would run for my life. Spending any time with that group would be absolute torture. And if heaven is filled with people like them, I thought, then I don't like their heaven. Surely Christendom is more than this pathetic bunch.

Michelle and I had gotten a bit more serious about our relationship, and she made it clear that if I wanted to continue to go out with her, I'd have to go to church with her. So I did. There were a lot of the boring, critical, judgmental Christian types there that were easy to despise, but there were also a lot of folks who had a special, genuine love flowing out of them; somehow, I knew that was God in them, and I had rarely experienced that before. Especially from Christians. Yet, there were quite a few of them here in this place. I was intrigued. I liked it. Then I found out the people at this church believed in healing and even prayed for each other, and sometimes God healed them. They even believed there could be miracles; imagine that. Then I found out they knew about angels and demons, and I thought, *Wow, maybe I've finally found some Christians who believe what I have experienced and known to be true.* I wanted to know more. Where did they get their beliefs from, and how is it that God's love is actually coming out of them?

One night as I was heading home on I-70, I was thinking about that church with the folks that believed in healing and had so much love that it oozed out of them. And all the great discussions that paved the way for me with Mike, the other diver at Casa Bonita. And what the guy had said to me about God not hearing you if you're not a Christian. I knew that was not true, the hearing part that is, because I had experienced Him so much all my life, but I thought that if making Jesus my savior would help my communication with Him be better then, that's what I wanted. All my life, I have wanted to know God better and have a better relationship with Him. So I simply said in my mind, *Okay, if this is really the right way to do things and what I've been told is true, then I accept You, Jesus, into my heart.* That was it; no fanfare, no flashing lights, no goosebumps or special feelings, nothing. But, somehow, I knew it was right. So that was it. I don't even know what night or week or month it was; I just know I did it, and it was somewhere between New Year's and St Patrick's Day. I do know the exact spot I was at during that moment, though; it was stopped like a picture for me; I can see it clearly in my mind's eye.

As the days went on, I noticed I felt cleaner, lighter and I really was hearing God better and beginning to notice all the different ways He communicated with me. I was seeing more and perceiving more about people and situations, and I had a strong desire to study and read the Bible. If I found something that was boring for me, I would pass it up and find something that wasn't. If I didn't do it that way, I found that it was impossible for me to read the Bible. By staying away from boring stuff and focusing on the not boring stuff, it actually expanded my tolerance of those other parts, and after a number of years, it got to where the boring stuff wasn't boring anymore, and I would get understanding and revelation no matter where I read. I also had to get a Bible with a good modern English translation so I could understand; otherwise, it was confusing and frustrating, and I found I would never read it.

I'm thankful that I was able to repent and that my sins are forgiven, and that I'm going to heaven, which I had no clue about when I asked Jesus into my heart. But that's okay; He taught me these things. It wasn't until after I asked Jesus into my heart to be my Lord and Savior that I came to understand that Jesus is the way the truth and the life and no one comes unto the Father except by Him (John 14:6). That revelation got bigger for me as I grew in my understanding of the Bible and the things of God. Sometimes I think we make it harder on people than it really is. That they have to know these things, or understand that, or do this, like John 3:16 (NIV) says, "For God so loved the world, that He gave His only begotten Son, that whoever believes in Him shall not perish, but have eternal life." I love the profound simplicity in that. And I love it that all we have to do is *believe*.

When I got baptized, I felt a power I had never known and a completeness that wasn't there before. I got baptized about a year later when I found out what it was. They had prayed for me before I got baptized that I'd also get the baptism of the Holy Spirt, which I believe happened. I didn't pray in the Spirit for another year or two, but I noticed an immediate increase in revelation and understanding any time I read the Bible. That was pretty neat.

I have a lot of compassion for people in other religions with other beliefs because I know that just like I was, that they are seeking God. They simply don't know what spirit they may be serving. And as always, the truth will set them free; the Lord always does it by way of the truth. And by love.

Confronted by a Bully

"[t]he kingdom of heaven suffers violence,
and the violent take it by force"
(Matthew 11:12, NKJV).

Our son was meeting friends downtown at a restaurant where they could sit outside and enjoy life. Winter was just ending, and the thought of enjoying the warm sunshine for a change appealed to them all. The place they had chosen was a comfortable spot, always fun and happy, full of interesting people glad to be off of work, and parking spots were easy to come by. As he made his way through the bar area, he noticed a couple of odd-looking guys standing there watching his friends, especially the girls, milling around enjoying themselves outside. Something felt very wrong about them, like they were sneaky with a devious intent, and the way they were watching his friends was downright menacing. He made eye contact with one of them, and the guy puffed out his chest and glared back, commenting with a "hey, what are you looking at" challenge.

Seeing a potential problem and wanting to avoid it, our son walked right over to him and said something like, "Nice day, how are you doing?" Then he reached out and shook his hand, which totally disarmed the guy, who then muttered something like "Yes, it is," then looked fleetingly down at the floor. Thinking all was now well that the situation had been defused, our son turned and went outside to greet the friends waiting for him on the patio.

Stepping into the sunshine, he clearly heard that still small voice deep inside that he had heard so many times before saying, "Don't look back, but that guy is going to come out after you. When he does, wait for him to get in your face, then head-butt him." That information was a little disconcerting. Especially when everyone was there for friendship and fun on this beautiful day, but if the confrontation happens, he thought, *At least I'll know what to do.* He stopped and pondered what he'd just heard, trying to wrap his mind around the thought that the Holy Spirit actually cared enough about him to tell him how to win a fight that hadn't even happened yet.

Joining in the laughter and the good conversation, the glaring man was soon only an afterthought. Later, after more people came and began settling into the chairs under the umbrellas, our son happened to look up just in time to see the glaring man making a beeline straight towards him. *Oh nuts, here goes the afternoon,* he thought to himself. The admonition about the head-butt flashed to the front of his mind. Sizing the guy up as he approached, our son could see he was bigger, looked strong, and outweighed him by at least forty pounds. The glaring man walked right up to our son and began loudly spewing hateful things so everyone outside could hear, about him and his friends, along with ample amounts of spit that he gleefully spattered all over our son's face. Then he just stood there smirking, obviously wanting to fight, thinking he had intimidated my son into submission.

Seeing a perfect set-up, my son slowly, very slowly, wiped the disgusting, dripping spit off his face without reacting, all the while noticing everything around them; the placement of the tables, position of innocent people, the exact distance between him and his adversary, and the astonished and appalled people who happened to see and hear what had just happened. He could see by his stance and the way he was holding his right arm and clenching his fist that the glaring man was definitely getting ready to punch.

Total silence fell like a blanket over the whole place. All eyes had turned in the direction of the commotion. Deep inside, he heard, *Now, do it now.* Then without any advance notice, before the bully could throw his punch, my son head-butted the glaring man right on the bridge of his nose with his forehead. Bam! Blood spurted out sideways as the creep pulled his head back in surprised agony. As his head came forward again, our son waited for the exact moment and got him one more time, driving his forehead again into the unsuspecting nose. The bully fell backward across the table behind him in too much pain to move.

The surprised audience was flabbergasted at what was taking place before their eyes. By their comments, they expected my son to have been torn into tiny pieces as the bigger guy had been threatening. Very threatening. Instead, the bigger guy lay in a mass of pain across someone else's table. My son then picked him up by his shirt collar and his belt, spun around to get enough momentum, and threw him over the little wrought iron fence onto the sidewalk outside the restaurant. The bully did a dead cat bounce, then lay squirming in a pool of his own body fluids shamed and humiliated on the cement. Looking up to see if he needed to defend himself against the friend attacking also, my son instead caught a fleeting glimpse of the coward's backside running quickly in the other direction. He chuckled to himself at the sight of another terrified bully running for cover.

Amazing how getting rid of the glaring bully and his perverted friend actually freed the whole restaurant from the cloud of oppression they brought with them. Everything was immediately more happy and free. The glaring man and his friend were nothing more than pompous bullies. They had been there for a while, intimidating people, making obscene comments towards the women, and the staff, for some reason, couldn't get rid of them. Their presence was uncomfortable, and everyone could feel it. Some knew why; others had no clue; they just knew something wasn't right. Now the whole place was free!

"He who has ears to hear let him hear!" (Luke 8:8, NKJV).

The Lord will use whatever situation we are in to help us and guide us. Even in the most difficult and unexpected things.

"I will be with you in trouble and rescue you" (Psalm 91:15).

That's quite a promise. And that's exactly what He did here with my son. He was training him to hear Him on the battlefield and beyond. We just have to do what He says, no more, no less.

If you have loved ones in the military or even the police or firefighters, wouldn't it help you to know they have practice hearing the Lord in hard situations, and they use that every day? That the training they got here in situations like this has actually prepared them for combat? That they bring others back with them safe and sound because they listened to the Lord and obeyed? It sure helps me with our sons. I know it has helped them and the men they are with just as it helped King David and his men when David got direction from the Lord and obeyed.

The Lord is also just as interested in helping mothers at home with their little ones as He is in helping His warriors. Or maybe you're in an office with lots of politics; if you listen to Him, He will help you to prevail no matter what you are doing. Nothing is too simple or too hard for Him to care about. If it matters to you, then it matters to Him. He can help all of us beat all the bullies in our lives.

Let me take it up a notch. Have you ever been confronted with a violent situation, an unprovoked violent situation? Have you ever had to use violence to counter their violence against you? Wouldn't you like to know what the Lord has to say to you for that specific situation and how to protect not only yourself but your loved ones? I would hope that you would. You see, this has not only happened to one son but to my wife, to me, and our other children as well.

The instances where we didn't hear God or listen to Him didn't go so well. But the ones where we did went exceptionally well, especially when we did what He said. In situations like these, you want to win, not just survive. As a matter of fact, you must win; others are depending on you whether you realize it or not. These confrontations can be terrifying, even traumatizing, especially when you don't know what to do and you're being hurt. Amazingly, many violent encounters are over in seconds. And another thing, you must actually be willing to do what the Lord tells you to do, be it run, hide, scream, punch, speak something specific, kick, scratch or head-butt, or maybe even do nothing. So make that decision now, that you will do what the Lord tells you to do, you will say what the Lord tells you to say. That decision now to be prepared for any potential situation in the future is the first step to winning.

"My Sheep Hear My Voice, and I know them, and they follow Me" (John 10:27).

The Bible says we can all hear His voice if we are Christians, and we can all learn to hear it better. If someone is not hearing it now, then now is a good time to start learning how.

Doesn't the Bible say that the Lord will protect us? Absolutely! But that doesn't mean that in every situation, you just stand there and do nothing. I can't tell you how many times He has delivered us from destruction by protecting us. His Word is true. But every situation is not the same. Sometimes there is an action that the Lord wants you to take, and if that's the case, I would suggest that you do it.

"It shall be, when you hear the sound of marching in the tops of the balsam trees, then you shall act promptly, for then the Lord will have gone out before you to strike the army of the Philistines" (2 Samuel 5:24).

More than anyone else, Christians don't want to talk about these things or even think about them, but I guarantee that many of us have had to deal with them already. We live in a real world with real violence, and the Lord knows what to do in absolutely every situation if we will just listen and obey. It works every time without fail.

Psalm 144:1
"Blessed be the Lord, my rock,
Who trains my hands for war,
And my fingers for battle."

Psalm 140:4 (NIV)
"Keep me safe, Lord, from the hands of the wicked;
protect me from the violent,
who devise ways to trip my feet."

"And from the days of John the Baptist until now the kingdom of heaven suffers violence, and the violent take it by force" (Matthew 11:12, NKJV).

Green Eyes

As far back as the ranchers in those parts could remember, folks had been tormented by a thing they called "Green Eyes." Sightings of the creature went as far back as the Indians before the barbed wire fences divided up the land. They called it Green Eyes because it only was seen at night, and its eyes shone a fluorescent green. They glowed in the dark, so there was never any question as to what it was. None of the cowboys would talk to outsiders about it. If you brought it up, they would just look away out across the vast prairie and change the subject. Or they'd just look at you without any expression crossing their faces, then turn and walk away. No comment, no explanation.

Our family has a couple of ranches here. Huge places. Places that spread out as far as you can see and then some. They have to be big, or they can't raise enough livestock to make a living. Water is scarce, and the New Mexican sun is relentless even in good years. Grass is sparse and cactus thrive, but only with a large spread is there enough to feed the animals. Just enough to make it in a bad year.

There's a beauty about the place, though—a rugged, harsh, and mysterious beauty. Sunrises and sunsets are incredible here; they create indescribable sights and colors that are truly breathtaking, the kind of sights you remember for the rest of your life. And because of the contrast between the light and the shadows, weird things take shape before your eyes that make you wonder. Then they slowly melt away as the sun moves across the sky—nothing supernatural, just fascinating and mysterious.

Every so often, you find a sinkhole right there in the pasture. Surprisingly there is an incredible labyrinth of caves and tunnels just beneath the surface, and the ground will fall in, making a hole and revealing the previously hidden tunnels and caverns. Some of the holes are just a few feet across, while others are as big as a football field. Most of the caves are impassable, while some go back quite a ways. They all have kind of an odd, mysterious air about them. After a good rain, one of the sinkholes becomes a big whirlpool that they say eventually ends up in Carlsbad Caverns hundreds of miles away and causes flooding there. It's amazing how connected those tunnels are.

When I was young, I found the most perplexing tracks going in and coming out of one of them. After showing them to some of the adults, they would scratch their heads and look around very bothered, then hurry back to the house. What were they? Let me just say that they are a mystery to this day.

This is a strange area, very strange in a spiritual sort of way. The amount of supernatural activity here is amazing. There are so many odd occurrences, so many weird things that I'm not going to tell them all. I'll highlight just a few.

Something about the Indians that lived here long ago, the ancient witchcraft and other things have made it ripe with a spiritual weirdness. And the power of some of these things is

big if you didn't know some of the scriptures like this one from
1 John 4:4 "[b]ut greater is He that is in us than he that is in the
world," you could feel pretty scared and helpless with all these
things around. There's a lot of comfort knowing that because
of Jesus, you have power over them, and they don't have power
over you. But it took us a while to get to that place of believing,
of understanding; it didn't happen overnight.

The main house had a ghost in the basement. I'd see it when
I'd go down there, and if all the beds were full upstairs for
some reason, I was always the one who had to go sleep in the
bed downstairs. I never liked it because the ghost would hover
above me as I laid there, and I would see it when I opened my
eyes and looked up. Somehow, I had this knowing, though, that
it couldn't touch me, so I wasn't afraid of it like most of the other folk were. But do you know how unnerving it is to try to sleep
with something hovering over you watching you all night? Ugh!
Many nights when you sleep on the main floor, you can hear
footsteps coming up the stairs from the basement; then, the
doorknob turns, the door opens, and no one is there. It's scary
and really freaky. Then you can hear footsteps walking across
the floor of the living room to the front door, which opens like
someone is going out, then it shuts. Sometimes I can see a figure there in the dark, and sometimes I can just hear it walking
and moving around. Regardless it's annoying and bothersome.
The relatives living there would always say, "Oh, it's just the
ghost." It also had an underlying wickedness that I could feel,
but I didn't know what could be done about it until a while after
I became a Christian.

After a number of years, I brought my family down for a visit. Sure enough, late into the first night, here came the ghost, like always. Michelle laid listening as it walked through our children sleeping soundly on the floor of the living room. I had never told her about the ghost on purpose. I didn't want her to be afraid or concerned for the kids. Besides, it didn't do it every night. She woke me up unsure and bothered, asking, "Hear that, who's walking through the house, who went outside and slammed the door at this time of night?"

I told her, "Oh, that's the ghost." I got mad as I realized there was something I could do about it. I had learned what to do. I had learned about the authority I had in Jesus. So I angrily commanded it to be bound and not return while we were there in Jesus' name. And you know what happened?

The steps stopped, and it left, and there was no more torment the whole time we were there. Neat, huh? The power in Jesus' name never ceases to amaze me.

My cousin Ron and my brother Mike had both had experiences with the ghost and more experiences with Green Eyes than anyone else. There are so many stories to tell, but I'll limit it to just a few.

Sometimes all you see are these green flashes of light nearby when you're driving or outside walking at night that showed you he was there. Other times you'd look out the window, and he'd be running right next to your truck even if you were going seventy miles an hour. You could slow down or speed up, and he'd still be there, then he'd simply disappear into the night. After a while, it started jumping into the back of Ron's truck and would cause it to sway back and forth across the gravel road until they thought they would lose control; then again, it would disappear, leaving them mad and terrified at the same time. Green Eyes was causing them such torment that they wanted to kill it. But how do you kill a spirit? They hated going through the gates in the pastures because many times, as they were either opening or shutting them, the thing would show up right next to them and scare the bejeebers out of them. My brother said it had an incredibly foul smell, was around eight feet tall, and would sometimes show these menacing teeth when they looked at it. Every time they saw him, they would shoot at him, and they said you could hear the bullets hitting its body; it didn't seem to do anything to it, but it always disappeared when they shot at it.

Turns out there were about three or four of them; they each had certain identifying features. One of them had one eye; they think my cousin shot it out one night. Never made sense, though, that you could affect something spiritual with something physical, but that's what seems to have happened. They both saw it happen when the shot was fired.

Other folks there have seen them at various times over many years, they were always scary and always intimidating, and they only saw them at night. And me? I never saw it with my eyes; I saw it in a dream once when I asked the Lord to show me if it was real, and if it was real, then what does it look like? It has a face that looks like it is so filled with hate and anger that it's incredibly dark and ugly, and the eyes shine with another worldly kind of green light. The stench coming off of it was like it carried the smell straight from hell. I thought to myself as I looked at it, *No wonder everyone is so afraid of this thing it's pretty scary to look at.*

We had learned a lot about the power in the name of Jesus, like the passage in Acts 3:16 where Peter says, "And on the basis of faith in His name, it is the name of Jesus which has strengthened this man whom you see and know; and the faith which comes through Him has given him this perfect health in the presence of you all."

And I also came across this passage in Hebrews 4:13 (KJV): "And there is no creature hidden from His sight, but all things are open and laid bare to the eyes of Him with whom we have to do." So I thought, *Wow, if God knows everything and can see it all and nothing is hidden from Him, then that means He knows about Green Eyes, and He knows what it is and where it is.*

So I just decided to bind him from ever bothering anyone down there again in the name of Jesus. I said it with great authority, great power, and intensity, and when I did, it felt like it had been done, that this thing would not be bothering my relatives anymore. I could feel the power and authority rise up from within me as I began to speak.

For a few years afterward, during phone calls, I would ask if anyone had seen Green Eyes, and they always said no. When we went down there about five years later, the answer was still the same. Imagine praying for something hundreds of miles away that was known to be very terrifying, intimidating, and spiritually powerful and had been around for centuries, and having your prayer actually work so well that it has been unseen for years. This really spoke to me about the power of God, the power of prayer even when it's short and simple, and the power of the Word. What an interesting and huge example this was for me and my family about what you can do.

This boosted my faith literally levels beyond where it was. So, for years now, if I have the authority to bind or cast out unwanted supernatural phenomena, I do. If I'm visiting a place, then I just bind it. It's best if I ask the Holy Spirit what to do in those situations. Everything is done in Jesus' name, of course, and sometimes other scriptures are added to it as the Holy Spirit leads. And you know what? It always works.

Peacemaker

This is a drawing I did of an encounter my brother and I had with a young red tail hawk.

Their nest sat behind us about four feet off the ground in the arms of a cactus and was a mishmash of wound baling wire, small twigs, animal fur, and feathers. It was big, at least three feet across. There were two babies, one had flown for the first time that morning, and this one flew the next day. He had obviously tried but couldn't yet because he was out of the nest and running around on the ground. Mama was circling not too far above us, watching her baby. He wasn't quite sure what to think of us. The other wing that you can't see is folded in place at his side.

The country in the background of the picture is where many of the encounters with Green Eyes occurred, the cave we explored is a few miles over the hills behind us, and the place with the ghost is back there out of sight to the right.

Stabbed in the Knee

We were playing football; I was about ten, school had just ended, and summer vacation had begun. I jumped high, straight into a small tree, to catch the overthrown pass, brought the ball down, and started to run. They tackled me when I landed back on the ground. But my knee hurt, I mean really hurt. Looking down, I saw that a small branch from the tree was sticking out of my leg. I grabbed it and pulled it out; it felt like it was scraping across every nerve in my leg; it was so painful. Turns out it had stabbed in between my kneecap and my joint. The pain was excruciating. I tried to continue with the game, but I couldn't, so I just limped home, the blood running down my leg.

I wasn't a Christian then, but I believed in miracles, and I believed in healing, which actually helped to take away a lot of the pain but didn't completely heal it yet. Fast forward twenty years. I had put up with the pain for that long. Many times, it wasn't painful; other times, I could hardly walk on it. It always felt like some of the bark from the wood had remained stuck behind my kneecap and like it would move here and there, always causing either discomfort or pain, and sometimes my knee would lock, and I couldn't move it. I actually dove competitively, climbed cliffs, and did gymnastics through high school and into college during this time. I could focus, and usually, the pain would leave. I was always determined to push through, though sometimes I could hardly walk. I just didn't want this to hold me back from enjoying life.

This was one of those times. I was selling real estate in Winter Park, Colorado, and many of the properties were condos on the second or third floor, with no elevator. I was walking by myself up a long, seemingly unending flight of stairs. My knee was so painful I couldn't make it to the top. I had been speaking healing to it for twenty years, a couple of those years as a Christian using the name of Jesus. But no real improvement. It was getting worse, and I didn't want to grow older and become one of those people that can't even walk up the steps to the house. Today, though, was different. I was mad. I was determined. So I stopped about halfway up, my knee now throbbing so bad I could hardly take it. And I said loudly and angrily, "Knee be healed in the name of Jesus!" then I screamed out, "Now!" And you know what? Something happened. The pain immediately left. Nothing felt different in my mind or in my heart, I didn't feel anything there at all, but my knee felt better.

I could hold up my leg and kick, and it didn't hurt. I could go up a few flights of stairs, and it didn't hurt. I could walk around in circles, which before when it flared up was too painful to do, but now there was no pain. Wow! An instantaneous healing. Or was it the accumulation of years of prayer? I don't know, and to tell you the truth, I don't care. All I know is that my knee was healed that day at that exact time, and it has been perfect for all the years since then. I do know that the power in the name of Jesus was the factor that made the difference.

So I would encourage you to speak healing over whatever ails you, in the name of Jesus. Yes, it took twenty years to get my healing, but you know what? I'm healed now and have been pain-free for years, and so can you. What if your healing happened in a moment like mine did? It's worth trying. It's worth putting forth the effort. Heck, you might just get healed!

I'm healed; stairs and steps don't bother me anymore.

Given a Few Businesses

Rocky Mountain Telecom

I stopped by to visit a friend of the family who was a stock-broker. In the course of the conversation, he mentioned some-one had come to him with a business idea about pay telephones. He said, "You know if you're interested, Greg, I'll pay for all the business expenses, and once you're up and running with a prof-it, you can pay me back. What do you think?"

"No contract, just a handshake." Twist my arm, I thought. We had just moved down from the mountains, and I needed to find work, so why not?

So I ran with it. He did what he said he would do, and I bought all the equipment, negotiated all the locations, found the right team to do the installs and maintenance, and began developing a nice network of payphones throughout metro Denver. I would pray for the Lord to open my eyes to see all the right locations and open the way to speak to the right people. Then I would drive all over looking for the right ones, and a spot would stand out to me, so I would pursue it, and usually, it turned out to be a good one. I called my new company Rocky Mountain Telecom.

For a while, the business looked like it was going to work well; things were moving right along, money was flowing in. But it reached a point where I could tell things weren't going to work out; it was odd, but I could sense a change in the spirit; I suppose it would be like saying I can feel a change in the wind, a strong change, I wished I could have done better, but the business climate was changing, and my gut (the Holy Spirit) let me know it was time to move on. As I would walk and pray at night, I started to get the knowing, not just the feeling, that the time was coming to an end and soon I would need to move on. I didn't want to. I wanted to grow the business as big as I possibly could and then sell it for a healthy profit, then move on with that money and start something else. But that knowing just got bigger and bigger each week that went by until there was no doubt that now was the time. No matter how much I didn't want to. So I decided I would sell everything and began looking for something else to do.

The people I had purchased all the stuff from in the first place said they would buy it all back, so I sold the whole business to them. What an incredible God appointment that was. It was a good deal for me but not enough to start something new and provide for my family at the same time. Within a month after I sold it, the value of that business began to diminish, and within six months, it was worthless. Wow, did I get out in time or what?

Then something started to show up that we had never seen before. They called them *cell phones*, and you could carry them with you and actually talk to people without a landline. I'm sure you know what happened from there; the rest, of course, is history. Thank God I obeyed His prompting, which in this case came in the form of a strong and then very strong knowing, and I was able to get out with a profit. It just goes to show that things are not always as they seem, and we can't count on something always being there. No matter how much we don't want it to change. The Lord knows the future. I made a decision long ago to move forward, accept the change, and become as proficient as I can in the new technology. Actually, I had to make that decision, or life was not fun. I always pray for wise progress in whatever I am doing. Things are going to be built; they are going to change whether we want them to or not, so why not pray that it all comes about with The Lord's guidance and with wisdom. It usually turns out much better for me that way.

Devil's Thumb Cross Country Ski Resort

We were living on Red Dirt Hill a few miles from the Winter Park Ski Resort. After helping my dad sell the family businesses, we had moved up there because I found a great job selling real estate out of Fraser. We found a good church and made a lot of new and wonderful friends, the closest of which were Mike and Mo. Now Mike and Mo lived in one of the cabins on a closed down cross-country ski resort called Devil's Thumb, as the caretakers. Their rent was free, and he really didn't have to do much to keep an eye on things.

According to the Indian legend, the name Devil's Thumb came from a fight between the devil and a mighty warrior. The mighty warrior won and buried the devil beneath a huge pile of rock and earth, leaving only his thumb showing up out of the rubble. So that every time we look at that large stone sticking up. The one they call Devil's Thumb. We are to be reminded that the devil has been defeated, and he and everything he stands for has been buried forever. Great story, don't you think? It seems the Utes had a revelation about Jesus before they even heard of Him.

We enjoyed visiting them there; the place was stunningly beautiful. Coming through the gate into the parking lot, the continental divide with the Devil's Thumb sticking up from it loomed majestically only a few miles to the east, the ranch sat in a flat valley on a huge meadow that stretched for over a mile along a creek running down the middle of it. A small, forested hill sat in the middle between this and another meadow almost the same size on the other side. Above the outbuildings to the west was a small mountain rising above the valley floor—five of the seven log cabins nestled at the base of it. The old two-story ranch house had been turned into a very quaint, fully equipped restaurant with a large deck out back overlooking the meadow.

There was a large log lodge with rustic but nicely appointed guest rooms and a great comfortable room for folks to relax in or read or play games and visit. Locker rooms for the guests and skiers were downstairs near the biggest jacuzzi I'd ever seen; the thing sat at least fifteen people. The large log ski shop had offices and more guest rooms upstairs and was fully equipped with rentals for about 225 people and had a treasure trove of all the ski attire, equipment, winter coats, and accessories anyone would possibly need.

Mike stabled his horses in the old barn nearby, and there were also Ski-Doos, tractors, and all the machinery necessary for a ski area stashed in it to protect them from the brutal mountain winters. Hidden in the trees nearby were another cabin and the old daycare facility that could also be used as a nice meeting room.

It had over sixty kilometers of cross-country ski trails and a training area with targets for the Olympic Biathlon skiers. Besides being breathtakingly beautiful, it was really quite the unique and incredible place.

One day Mike says, "Hey Greg, I've been thinking about it, and I believe we could reopen the whole resort and be successful at it." He was a carpenter, and yes, I had run a hotel with restaurants, but a whole huge resort?

It seemed overwhelming, too hard, and besides, I'd never done anything like this before, so I told him, "No."

He smiled and said, "Well, think about it for a while because I don't know what to do either, but I think that together we could make it work."

Every day for the next couple of weeks, it would come to mind often, and I would go through all the buildings in my memory, and all I could think about was how I didn't know what to do and that it would be way too hard. I could see the great potential of the place; I just couldn't see past my inexperience and lack of knowledge. Finally, during the week before Christmas, I was minding my own business when I heard an audible voice tell me, "If you pass this up, you will regret it the rest of your life," just like it had said concerning marrying Michelle. When I heard that, I looked around to see who had said it and of course no one was there. Then I realized, *Oh, this is the Lord again; I guess I need to rethink things.*

So, if the Lord is telling me to do this, then that means I can, and I'll know what to do. Hmmm, I also don't want to go through life regretting that I missed out on a God-ordained opportunity and wondering what would have happened if I had at least tried. Well, I guess I'd better do it. But the guess "I'd better do it" part took a day or so to sink in. It took that long for the knowing to sink in that I should at least try. But once it did, once I was committed in my heart to trying, along with the knowledge that God was in it, then and only then did the peace come. Once the peace settled in my heart, it calmed my mind, and I knew I could do this thing I'd never done before. I wasn't afraid of failing anymore. So I called Mike up and said, "Okay, I'm in."

And he starts yelling, "Praise God, praise God. Today was the deadline we gave the Lord believing that if nothing happened, we wouldn't do it, and if something did happen, then it was of God. We knew you were the only one that could do this; God showed that to us; we're so glad you said yes; you won't regret it." *Well, that was quite the unexpected reception,* I thought to myself. I didn't realize how much they really believed in me.

This was on the Monday after Christmas. We called the owner and told him we wanted to reopen the resort, and we'd give him a small percent of what we made. We couldn't promise a certain number as we had no clue what would happen, and the place had been closed for a season or two. Amazingly he was totally for whatever we wanted to do; no debate, no argument, no bartering. We agreed on 10 percent of net profits, and all we had to do to begin was get insurance on the place. It was basically a handshake agreement over the phone. We worked a contract out over the next few days. Mike knew an insurance agent who took care of it for us that day for a small partial premium and a lawyer who had us incorporated by Wednesday with another handshake promise we pay him by spring. We opened a business bank account with $100. The power was kept on by the owner to keep the place from freezing up, so we just took over that bill, and the phone line had never been disconnected, so we had the original number.

We walked through each building to assess what we had and where to start. Turns out we had everything we needed already, even the linens for the bedding and silverware for the restaurant and all the cabins were completely furnished. We lacked nothing. I looked at Mike and said, "Well, all I have to do is learn how to run the cash registers and write up the rental forms; how about you figure out the phone system, and we'll be good to go." We figured, well, it's Wednesday, and if that's all we need to do, let's open on Friday, two days later. So we did. No advertising, no employees, no business plan, $100 to start with, and no borrowed money, still didn't know everything we needed to know, but we did it anyway. Just five days from "okay, let's do this to opening day."

By the end of that weekend, I had hired a chef for the restaurant, and a couple who had worked there before to groom and maintain the trails, so I made them the designated ski patrol also. I got them a couple of certifications, and they were good to go. By Sunday, we had reservations for people who called out of the blue from as far away as Australia and France, and we had made over $1,000 just in the ski shop. Not bad for a first weekend, and having to figure it all out as you go, don't you think?

After a week, things were running so smoothly that Mike decided to keep his day job as a construction supervisor, so I ran the whole thing and handled the ski shop until I was able to hire some more folks to help out. By the end of the second week, I had a competent, full crew in every department. No advertising; God just brought them to us. I'd be working and look up, and here would be another person wanting to be a part of things. Mo helped oversee the lodge office and answer the phone, and Michelle was pregnant with baby number two and helped out where she was needed when she was able.

Turns out all my fears about not knowing what to do or being unable to do it were unfounded. All I had to do was look at a situation, and I already knew what to do; it was amazing and wonderful. I had the wisdom and understanding, and I didn't even know it before it was already there. My beliefs about what I could and could not do were wrong, and I didn't even know it. I simply needed to step out of my box, my comfort zone, and just try. Though it's so simple to say that, it's a whole other thing to actually do it. I had to change my beliefs about myself, I had to get rid of a fear of failure and not let it control my thinking or my actions and choices, and that was not easy. But once I made the decision to "just do it" and started to "just do it," all that fear melted away.

By the end of January, we realized because of the seasonality of the business that we had to make a year's income in four months. We were making good money, enough to pay everything and begin savings to carry the place for the rest of the year. The lodge had people every night, all the cabins were full, the ski trails were well maintained, and people had nothing but praise for the food and service in the restaurant.

Looking a few months ahead to the summer, we decided that rather than hay the meadow, we'd lease it to a nearby rancher to graze his cattle, and I found an outfit that would do chuckwagon dinners and hayrack rides as long as there was no snow on the ground, and we'd take a fair percentage from their income.

Mike and I were sitting on the deck of the restaurant overlooking the meadow on the last day of March, enjoying the sunny weather and watching the people enjoy themselves, and he says, "You think it would be too hard to do a race here?"

"No, I think it would be pretty easy. What kind of race are you thinking about?"

"A Cross Country Ski race, and what if we could have it start here and finish somewhere in Winter Park?"

"That would work if we could get permission from some of the landowners to get there. You know we still have good snow, but the season is winding down, so we have to do it sometime between now and before the snow melts. It's the end of March, so if we do it within two weeks, even if it's warm every day, we ought to still have enough snow to cross country ski on, don't you think?

"Okay, let's see who's land we have to cross and where a good ending spot would be. If we're going to do this, we only have two, maybe three weeks; do you think we can pull it off?

"Let's try. Okay." So we prayed and asked God to guide us, and off we went to put something else together we'd never done before.

We found out that if we made a barbed wire gate at the end of the property by the road, then we could go through the Idlewild property all the way to Beaver Lodge and end right about their parking lot near the main road. Everyone was in agreement, which was wonderful, so I had our people forge the trail clear to Winter Park. Turns out it wasn't quite long enough for a proper race, so we decided to have the racers go around a few loops on our trails before heading over towards Idlewild, which made it more interesting and challenging for the racers anyway.

"Now we need to name this thing, so what should we call it?"

"Well, it ends up in Winter Park, and it will benefit the whole community if we can get enough of them to embrace it as more than a race but a community celebration. So I said let's call it the Winter Park Spring Fling because that's where it is and when it is, and it's like the last fling before spring and summer start."

"Okay, I like that," Mike replied.

The neighbors timed the sanctioned races at Winter Park and offered to set up the finish line and time everyone in our race when they found out what we were doing. Wow, that was neat, so we made sure our trail was the right distance so the racers would have valid competition times they could turn in.

We were hoping for fifteen to twenty-five racers to start with. That seemed reasonable, seeing how we only had three weeks to put this thing together and notify people. We figured we could round up at least that many locals and call it successful. But something unexpected happened. By the end of the first week, we had one hundred people already registered, and fifteen of them were Olympic and pro-level athletes. So now what do we do? I know let's have two races, an amateur and a pro-level race, so we can separate them, and we'll present awards for first, second, and third for each group.

By race day, we had 200 amateurs and about thirty-five pro racers. Mike and I stood there astonished at how this whole thing came together in just three weeks as we watched the first wave of skiers leave the starting line behind the ski shop. It was so satisfying for us, even exhilarating. The whole race went incredibly smoothly and came off without a hitch. As I presented the awards and shook hands with the winners, I was still in awe at what we had accomplished in such a short period of time. We knew it was God's idea that He had ordered things for us; we just had to do our part, follow His leading, and put it together without worrying about the short time frame. Praise the Lord for witty and clever ideas that work!

You know that was in April of 1984. As I write this, it's many years later, and Winter Park has continued with the race and festivities very successfully ever since. And to think I almost turned this whole opportunity down because, at first, I didn't believe I could do it. And to also think that the whole thing was just given into our hands. Amazing!

With ski season over, Mike and Mo now felt the Lord had called them to go start a work they called Lighthouse Ministries on the island of Grenada that summer. They began immediately after the island was freed from the Communists. Their ministry started with all the unwanted children and those whose families had been destroyed and were now forced to live on the streets. There were so many miracles and profound changes in the kids' broken bodies and broken lives that the adults on the island were amazed and began to come and see for themselves.

Asking, "Who is this Jesus these kids are talking about that heals people and sets them free?"

So I took all the money I had saved for the business for the next season, about $30,000, and gave it to Mike to help them get started down there. He bought an old run-down colonial home with lots of land, renovated the home, built a church, erected a huge satellite dish, created a state-of-the-art TV and recording studio, and became a down station for TBN, Trinity Broadcasting Network, and broadcast their programming across the Caribbean and parts of South America. He called it Lighthouse TV Grenada. In the 1990s, with the help of Bob Nichols of Calvary Cathedral International in Fort Worth, Texas, and Paul Crouch, Mike was able, through a series of miraculous, God-ordained, circumstances to also help found Lighthouse TV Uganda, which is operating there to this day. Bob was Mike's beloved mentor and friend, and he supported and guided, and counseled him from the start.

The next time Paul Crouch, the founder of TBN, came down, he said to Mike, "You know this really is a miracle; the fact that you can even broadcast is a miracle."

"Yes, I agree," Mike said, smiling.

"No, Mike, it's a bigger miracle than you think. I just noticed your satellite dish is facing the wrong direction, and you're still able to get the signal!" Turns out Mike also had an unknown but truly incredible gift to create and produce TV programming. He won a number of Angel Awards for it before he succumbed to an untimely death in 2001.

I suppose my whole point with all of this is that without Devil's Thumb as a springboard, none of this would have happened the way it did. Mike would remind me of that often. We never know the consequences of our decisions until we see them play out. For me, this was definitely a good decision. I'm glad I listened to the Lord on this one. It ended up touching many more lives than I'll ever know.

CE Inc.

My mother brought a cousin over for dinner that I'd never met or even heard of before. He was a first cousin from her mom's side of the family. By the time the meal was over, he had offered to help me start a business that he would fund completely if I would just come to New Mexico and look his operation over and the competition as well and then make a decision. I said no because it was a convenience-type store that had a large high-end tobacco aspect to it, and I didn't really want anything to do with tobacco.

In America's Christian community, we many times mistakenly consider tobacco and alcohol as the two worst sins you can commit, then after that, of course, fall murder, rape, adultery, theft, and so on. So, I didn't want any part of it. The judgment from fellow believers would be huge, and I didn't want to put myself in that position. I simply didn't want to have to deal with it. And besides that, Michelle and I don't smoke and couldn't stand to be around those who did. It was annoying. But somehow, we were intrigued and agreed to at least look at the various operations before making a final decision.

I was shocked on our trip to find out that most of the people I met that were involved with tobacco all the way from farming to the final product were Christians. And most of them had been making a living like this for generations. None of this fit into my little American Christian box, and I was being forced to think outside my own little world again. Imagine that!

I agonized for a few weeks over the decision. I scoured the Bible for answers and advice. My beliefs were rocked as I found out what the Word really said about sin and the various things that were considered a sin by the Lord. I asked pastors to show me where tobacco would be a sin. They couldn't. The passage about sinning against your body had to do with sexual sin. The only thing that came close was that alcohol was actually allowed (even Jesus and the apostles drank wine), but there were very clear warnings not to get drunk. Other Christians also brought up gluttony, but that was another instance where we all must eat; just don't make it a habit of eating all the wrong things or eating too much. Pretty simple, really.

I realize that some folks will disagree with me, but the Bible clearly addresses things like lust, jealousy, gossip, pride, idolatry, covetousness, stirring up strife, acts that physically hurt people, and sex outside of marriage, and so on. Unbelief is considered a huge sin by the Father. I found out that there were things I was calling sin that weren't and things that God calls sin that I didn't consider a problem. Now I had to decide what to believe, my culturally wrong beliefs, or what the Bible said, which also meant I would have to change the way I thought about a number of things which was not easy. How sad that we get all bent out of shape over something that isn't even worth fighting about. How wrong I had been in some of my beliefs. I wanted really badly to find something to justify my thinking that tobacco was a sin, but it just wasn't there. It's pretty obvious that health-wise, it's not best for us, but it's also not a sin. I realized the other great concern of mine was being ostracized and condemned by fellow Christians. Which, of course, did happen later in spades. Interestingly during the weeks where I had to make my decision, we met many more Christians that were for our business than were against it, and not one of them smoked. I think that it was God's grace for me to help me make the right choice.

So, I said yes, and we had an incredibly successful business for nine years. With this venture, I wanted to design the business in such a way that I could create a good life for me and my family. I wanted to control it; I didn't want it controlling me. I didn't want just another job.

I had to refine the way I make choices and decisions, so they lined up with my vision for this business and my family, so they lined up with my beliefs. The kids were still young, eleven, ten, and eight when we started. I saw almost every game they played in and was at most of the events that were important to them. Because I ran my business, and it didn't run me, I was also able to do many things we had never been able to do before. This wouldn't have been possible if I had worked the business as just another job, day in and day out—what a concept.

I designed the systems at the start to be simple and effective, and at the same time, we built the business up to where we could easily afford to hire some other folks to help. Then I spent all the time necessary to train the managers and the crew to run things as I wanted. I gave them authority to make any decision that was customer-oriented within a few easy-to-follow guidelines. It gave them much more freedom in their job, which made them happier, and it freed me from making decisions I didn't really need to be making. By doing it that way, the place ran like a clock, whether I was there or not. Then I was able to work a few hours a day and be successful in business and with my family at the same time.

The Lord showed me that the guys in the Old Testament that sat at the gate as elders and judges couldn't have done that if they didn't have things running well in their businesses first. I hadn't thought of it like that before, that my business could be the support necessary to do other important things I wanted to do. I knew sometimes other people could do that; I just never thought that I could actually do it myself. I don't know why I just didn't. Once I changed that belief from I "could never do that" to "yes, I can do that," then I could, and I did. It's so amazing how our beliefs drive what happens to us.

To make it work, I simply had to follow the admonitions in Proverbs 24:27, 27:23: "Prepare your work outside, and make it ready for yourself in the field, afterwards, then build your house...Know well the condition of your flocks, and pay attention to your herds..."

Once I got the business working right, I knew I would be able to spend the time with my family and doing other things. So I put in all the extra hours and necessary effort and focused on making that happen. Once I created that foundation, I was able to transition easily to the next level. Also, because of the systems and checks and balances I had in place, it was easy to know the condition of things any given day and take care of any issues as soon as they cropped up. Many times I was able to see them before they happened and deal with them then, so they never became an issue.

Even though the other businesses around us and the neighborhood liked and supported us, we still had some enemies—other Christians and Satanists. The Satanists hated us because God was with us, and lives were being healed and changed, and the kingdom was being expanded. They would come one, two, or three at a time, sometimes dressed very weirdly, and usually walk counterclockwise in circles around our free-standing drive-thru building, speaking out curses and stopping occasionally to perform rituals against us. Some mornings we would arrive to find things representing curses and sacrifices laying at the front door. We were not afraid because of the blood of Jesus and the power of His Word, which work every time.

A few specific Christian churches, on the other hand, hated us for one reason and one reason only, because we sold tobacco, which was what I was concerned about in the first place—the judgment from other Christians. But the Lord told me not to let that bother me, don't take it to heart. It took me a little while to get past their offenses; I mean, we're supposed to be on the same side. And besides that, every convenience store in America sells tobacco, lots of tobacco; what's wrong with these people?

They were ruder, more violent, and much more obnoxious than the Satanists. They would actually come and stand and scream death curses and condemnation against our business through the drive-thru window and tell my people they were going to hell, all while customers were in the store. They would even scream and yell at the customers getting out of their cars. Says volumes about their version of Christianity, doesn't it? No wonder folks resent Christians. Again, we were not afraid because of the blood of Jesus and the power of His Word, which work every time. Even against curses formed by other Christians.

Amazingly, Jesus touched the hearts of a number of the Satanists and turned their lives around when they came into our store. One of them even had a favorite T-shirt that he always wore when he came by, "Christian Death," It had a picture of a demonic man stabbing a Christian with a butcher knife. After his heart was changed, he came by often because he liked talking to us. But those other Christians? They were very ugly, had bad breath, and sadly, their hearts were hearts of stone.

When I established the business, the Lord said we were the gatekeepers here. We were to improve the area through prayer and keep the blight from downtown from coming past a certain line into Lakewood. I had to study to find out what a gatekeeper really was and what the responsibilities were. Since it was important to the Lord, I wanted to do my job well.

The area had once boomed with life but now had become run down with lots more crime when we moved in, and the blight was moving quickly and getting worse. So for nine years, we prayed there six days a week, and it made a difference for the area; we could tell within the first month that things around us were starting to improve. Things were already starting to look and feel cleaner, and the crime was subsiding and going back beyond the line that we drew. There were so many amazing and incredible things that happened within the business. I don't have room here to mention all the healings, lives changed, hearts and minds healed, and even miracles. I can't tell you how many people God delivered from smoking in our shop.

By the time we left, whole city blocks around us had already begun to be revitalized with strong, vibrant new businesses moving in and more to be cleaned up and renewed in the near future. New churches were cropping up nearby and being established, where the pastors prayed with me and not against me for the area, the people, and the businesses in our community. We had done our job; the kingdom was advancing, new boundaries had been set. I turned the responsibility of gatekeeper over to those pastors. It was time to move on.

So these are a few of the businesses that the Lord has given me. I expected God to move, but I never expected any of them to come to pass like they did, nor did I expect them to be the type of business that they were. It was always a surprise, an amazing surprise. One thing I did do before each of them came to pass was to pray in the Spirit a lot. And I would speak specific scriptures over myself, my family, and our lives. I know that helped.

I also almost lost two of these opportunities because I didn't think I could do it or didn't like what it was, though neither were illegal or immoral. Because of these and other instances, I have learned never to discount the package an opportunity presents itself in; it must be opened and looked at. Sometimes I already know what to do with it; other times, I have to look further, think it through, and ask the Lord what to do with it. Then be willing to do what He says. Sometimes it's a yes, sometimes it's a no.

I don't want to miss out because I did not recognize the time of my visitation; I didn't recognize it was an opportunity from the Lord. Sometimes my lack of vision held me back; from Luke 19:44.

I also didn't want to miss an opportunity because I'm listening to the wrong voice as we are admonished over and over that "he who has an ear let him hear what the Spirit says to the churches." I want to hear what the Spirit has to say; I don't want to miss out because of unbelief, preconceived ideas, or wrong thinking; I want to know the truth.

"Behold, I stand at the door and knock; if anyone hears My voice and opens the door, I will come in to him, and will dine with him, and he with Me" (Revelation 3:20).

When He's offering an opportunity, I now want to say yes even if I don't understand it yet because I know He only gives good gifts to us. And like it says in 1 Timothy 6:17, that He richly supplies us with all things to enjoy. I know that the opportunity He's offering will even be something that not just benefits me but is something that I can enjoy. Nice!

The Bomb

"Train up a child in the way he should go,
even when he is old he will not depart from it"
(Proverbs 22:6, NKJV).

From the time our kids were little, we made decisions, even difficult ones, and included them. We wanted to teach them how to think through things and how to come to good conclusions. We would lay out the circumstances and the options as we saw them, then ask them what they thought and how they would handle it. What's wonderful is that many times they were hearing directly from God, and their ideas were the best answer for the situation, even as small children. No one was allowed to criticize or judge anyone else's answer. That way, it was safe, they could make mistakes with no condemnation, and they all could learn. That way, they could grow in their confidence, and their answers constantly improved. To this day, many years later, they will call us up, give us the particulars and the options, and we will bounce things off of each other until the best decision is made.

We did the same with prayer. When we asked God for wisdom or guidance, we would pray and then ask them what the

Spirit told them or what they heard. They grew up asking the Lord for wisdom and hearing His answers, then acting on them. They learned to know when it was God and when it wasn't. That also translated into relationships with other people. They know when someone is real or not; they just know. So now, as adults, it's a part of their daily lifestyle.

Fast forward to a difficult military situation, our son was in the middle of defusing a bomb; it was a test, and it was a complicated mess of wires and odd parts. All of his common sense and all of his training said one thing, but the Spirit of the Lord was saying another. The battle in his mind about what was right and what to do was so intense he had to stop for a moment, take a deep breath, and separate which was his thinking and which was the Lord, then make a decision. Time is ticking away, and there won't be much left if things blow up. Going against everything he had been trained to do, everything that he knew was right, he went with what the Lord was telling him and was successful. His years of practice listening for wisdom and answers from the Lord was now being used to save lives. The procedure was unorthodox by EOD Standards, but it worked. During the debriefing, as he explained why he did what he did, everyone was amazed at the "why" because it was something none of them had ever known or thought of doing; it was new, it was unconventional, they understood it, they liked it, and it worked well.

My sons also found that listening to the Lord helps with combat, clearing houses, going on patrol, and other life-threatening encounters. Such as, "Careful, there's an ambush behind that door," or "This nice lady is leading you into a trap," or "Those kids playing are a distraction for the terrorists behind them," or "Those dangerous-looking men are for you, they are on your side."

"Fathers, do not provoke your children to anger, but bring them up in the discipline and instruction of the Lord" (Ephesians 6:4).

May the hearts and ears of those who are reading this be opened to hear and know the truth in all their situations, in Jesus' name.

Over the Waterfall Backward

It was a beautiful Colorado summer day, so I decided to rent some kayaks and take the boys to an easy place to play around and learn how to paddle them. Pulling up to the gate, I saw a sign saying the area was closed for road work. Nuts. Now, where? So I drove to another place nearby that looked good. From the place where we would start to the point where it disappeared around the mountain, it looked perfect. Going around to the other side of the mountain, I noticed there was about a mile stretch that was also perfect. The only problem was a small stretch that we couldn't see where it went as it flowed around the bend of the mountain.

A cardinal rule for canoeing or kayaking is to know the water you will be on before you get on it. So unless someone else that you trust has run that part of the river, it's important to check the whole thing out to make sure it's doable and safe. I estimated there was about a quarter of a mile that we couldn't see; the rest was quite nice. After carefully checking out all the parts we could see, I decided it all looked so good that it was okay to take a chance and go for it.

Travis would be the first to go with me. We pushed out from the shore into the easily flowing stream, and I began teaching him how to paddle and various things to look for about how the water moved. Garrett followed on a wild game path along the side as we went.

Downriver, just beyond the curve where I could see good at the start, the water began speeding up and started to get rougher. As we floated along and I was trying to teach Travis more about what to do, the water got even faster and rougher. It quickly became fast enough and rough enough that there was no way I could help him to the bank to safety. If things didn't change back quickly to the smooth and easy parts I had seen, we were going to be in trouble, and there was not much I could do to help my son.

At first, I helped him keep his kayak pointed down the river, so he could move along with me and also not tip over, that is, until the water became so furious, it was starting to throw us around. Not good. Now, what do I do? I simply yelled out, "Jesus, Jesus, Jesus." But now, I was twenty feet in front of him, working to keep myself from flipping over. Looking up just in time, I see a small two-foot waterfall directly in front of us. I straighten my kayak out to go over it, and at the same time, I'm trying to yell above the noise of the rapids at Travis to warn him and help him straighten his kayak too. But he couldn't hear me above the sound of the now raging river. My heart went into my throat for my son as I shot over the small waterfall. I had to focus now on getting myself safely through this mess before I could even think of helping him. I couldn't very well help him if I was upside down underwater or dead.

I was so determined to make it through to where I could help him that I suddenly felt myself infused with strength as I easily navigated the raging water. But now I see another waterfall, and this one is bigger, about three or four feet. I kept myself straight through the rapids as we sped downriver so I could at least hit the waterfall straight on and hopefully make it successfully. As I crested the top and shot out and down, my heart leaped again because it was bigger and farther down than what I could see. The kayak hit the water nose first, and I went completely underwater then popped quickly up. The skirt to keep the water out popped off because it was old, so my kayak immediately filled up, and I was riding just below the surface. I was now in trouble; I couldn't maneuver over to the bank. Actually, I could hardly maneuver at all. At least I was still facing straight forward.

I looked back to see how Travis was doing. The first waterfall had turned him sidewards, and he was going perfectly straight backward over the second one. Nuts! He hits the churning water below and goes under and sidewards. "Jesus, Jesus help us!" I cry out. After a short, while he popped up from underneath, and he was okay. He had struggled mightily to get out and above water for a breath. I was so greatly relieved to see him make it back to the surface.

I turned my attention forward again just in time for a third waterfall, but this one seemed kind of big. I prepped as well as I could in a partially submerged kayak and crested the falls. Oh no! It was a ten-foot drop. I breathed in deeply and held my paddle above my head as I dove into the raging, churning water at the bottom. Once I hit, the power of the churning water shot me out and to the right side of the river into shallower water and some big rocks.

Pushing with all my might to get out of the kayak before I was dragged upside down through the rocks, I cleared the surface just in time to look back and see Travis.

He and his kayak were crashing over the large falls into the raging, white, foamy water; he went under again but quickly popped up out of the water, his kayak flowing downstream without him.

As you can tell, this is not turning out very well.

I made a decision based on what I could see, and what I could see was quite good. I assumed that the part I couldn't see would be similar to the other parts of the river. But the very small part that I couldn't see turned out to be a game-changer; it wasn't even close to what the rest of the visible river was. If not for God's grace, we could have died that day.

I judged that situation based on most of the information. I judged it on everything I knew from what I could see. Because I had most of the information, I chose to assume that what I couldn't see would be similar to what I could. Boy, was I wrong. So wrong that we ended up in not just a bad situation, but a potentially deadly one. I was only missing a small piece of the puzzle to make my assessment complete, so it seemed logical that based on the other things I knew, that this would be similar. But it wasn't. It wasn't even close.

My decision, my assumption, my judgment, my assessment of the situation based on most, but not all of the information was so bad, so wrong that it almost hurt us, it almost cost us our lives. Just one tiny piece of information was missing. It just so happened that it was the most critical piece, and had I known, I would never have gone forward with my plan. I would never knowingly jeopardize the well-being of my children or myself. Yet I did. This time I did, with almost devastating consequences. All over one, small, unknown piece of information. And the assumption that because everything else I can see, everything else I know from that, means that the part I don't know and can't see will be similar.

My information was good but not complete. It was not accurate because it wasn't complete. In Hosea 4:6 (KJV), it says, "My people are destroyed for lack of knowledge." How true that was for this situation.

But there is another thing involved here too. I broke a cardinal rule for running a river by choosing to attempt it without a complete knowledge of that stretch of the water. There are certain rules, certain standards in life that should never be broken. It's like taking off in an airplane without a thorough check of all the systems and just assuming they will all be okay. That's a cardinal rule that should never be broken.

How many times do we all make decisions about things with only some of the information? Or judgments about people without first hearing all sides. And how many times are we wrong? Yet, we will even defend our bad decision because some, not all, of the facts were correct. That's silly.

There are many times in our daily lives that we must make decisions or judgments on things and situations without all the facts. I'm not talking about these. I'm talking about certain crucial, key, or pivotal decisions that can have life-changing consequences if we decide something without accurate information.

I made that mistake that day, but I can guarantee that I will never do it again, and neither will my sons, who went through it with me.

So, how did this whole thing turn out? Well, let me tell you.

Another one hundred feet or so from the big waterfall was a huge, terraced waterfall checkered with boulders of all sizes and broken, splintered trees that went down at an angle for about fifty yards. It was a death trap. Then between that waterfall and the one we'd just fallen over was a tree that had fallen all the way across the river. Its branches had been stripped and made it look like huge, sharp, menacing teeth that went from the tree down into the water; no way under that either. But thankfully, it forced us to the banks of the river, me on the far side where my kayak had been thrown, and Travis to the near side where Garrett had been walking and witnessed the whole ordeal.

Struggling in the strong current was very hard, but Travis had to make it to the bank without getting caught in the teeth of that fallen tree, or worse, being sucked over the deathtrap waterfall. I stood in the cold, knee-deep water and watched helplessly as my son made an incredible herculean effort to survive, to get to safety. Miraculously he made it to where Garrett could help him and the kayak up out of the water. They were about sixteen and fifteen at the time.

Seeing that Travis was safe, I turned to get my kayak and get to the other side of the river. But the current was so strong that it was stuck sidewards against the rocks at the bank, and I couldn't move it. I heaved and pushed and pulled, and it wouldn't budge. The water was cold enough that my feet were starting to get numb. I thought to myself, *I'm really in trouble now.* Oh, I never mentioned that I was recovering from a back operation and was supposed to be taking it easy. I know, I know; Michelle reminds me what a stupid decision I made every time this comes up. But now, she doesn't say anything; she just gives me that look. Actually, as I write this, she has had to forgive me all over again.

Anyway, I could feel the fear that I wouldn't make it pounding me upside the head. I was tired, I was hurting, and I was so mad and ashamed that I had made such a bad decision that I could hardly stand myself. I just stood up, raised my hands towards the sky, and said, "Lord forgive me, I am so sorry; I repent for this incredibly bad decision. I need Your help, I'm worn out, and I can't make it to the other side myself, and my sons can't help me. You promised to help us and rescue us, and I desperately need Your help now. Show me what to do and help me do it."

I felt a strong impulse to try to move the kayak again. So I got a good grip, pulled, and up it came so easy it felt like I didn't do anything, but that it just came up on its own. Amazing! Thank You, Jesus! Then I dumped the water out of it; now to get back to the other side. There were only about twenty yards between me, the tree with teeth, and the deathtrap waterfall, and I probably had about twenty-five yards across the roaring current to get to the bank on the other side.

I tried to yell above the thunder of the water so the boys knew what I was doing. It was too loud, and none of us could hear each other. They had been watching carefully as I got myself ready to sprint across the river without going over the next waterfall. Pointing the kayak directly at the other side and using sign language to show them what I intended, I got in my seat, got the paddle ready, said, "Jesus, I know You'll help me do this," and pushed with all my might into the rushing water. Using everything within me, I made the best of every stroke and surged across towards the other side.

About midstream, the power of the raging water began to take me towards deathtrap waterfall, but I wasn't about to give up; I kept up the paddling and just said, "Jesus, Jesus." Once I was about eight feet from the bank, Travis jumped into the water to rescue me. They caught me just before I was taken over the falls. He had one hand holding the rope on the front of the kayak and his other being held tightly by Garrett, who was halfway in the river, pulling us in towards the bank. It was a heroic effort that took supernatural strength and incredible courage. What a relief, we were all holding our breath for a desperate moment. But we made it. Safe at last!

I knew better than to make a decision to go down the river without accurate and complete information. Yet I did it anyway. I have never made such a bad decision before by violating a cardinal rule. I will never make that mistake again. Ever! Thank You, Father, for Your grace and Your mercy and for saving us even after I made such a bad decision, even after I put us all in harm's way. Thank You, Father, for delivering me even from my own foolishness.

As it is written: "He sent His word and healed them And delivered them from their destructions" (Psalm 107:20, KJV).

May any who are reading this be delivered from any bad decisions you have made, from anything that was foolish, anything destructive, and may the Lord rescue you, deliver you, restore you and bless you in Jesus' name.

Bad Food,
Bad Service

Have you ever gone to a restaurant and had a bad meal or bad service or both? I'm sure a lot of folks can relate. But what if you had five in a row? I mean bad food and bad service five times in a row. Five meals in a row.

Those of you know how it is when you have kids. You've been traveling way too long without a break for them to get out and run around. They are tired, they are hungry, so they're a bit cranky, and you pull into a restaurant that looks like it will work for your family. The service is slow and scattered. When the food comes, it's not what you ordered; then, when you send it back and get something close to what you ordered, it's so bad it's disgusting; the kids are now crying because they're so hungry and tired. Your spouse is upset, you're upset, things seem to be spiraling down fast. This is definitely not the enjoyable, happy outing you had hoped for.

We were on vacation going to Yellowstone National Park so the kids could see the geysers, all the wildlife, and the bubbling hot pools of water that spring right out of the ground. There's nothing like it anywhere else in the world. So we stopped at five separate places as we traveled along the way, and things were bad at each place. In fact, they seemed to be getting worse. I mean, what are the chances of getting bad food and service five times in a row? Granted, each place gave us our meals for free, but that's not much consolation when everyone is still hungry; we still all need to eat something. So we did—hot dogs, candy bars, popcorn, and potato chips, and energy bars that tasted like cardboard. Okay, so it wasn't the best diet, but it satisfied the kids until we could hopefully get a decent meal at the next destination. Which, of course, didn't happen.

It was starting to get painful. Something is very wrong. It's like there's this curse or something everywhere we go to ruin our trip. And this was supposed to be fun.

We spent the night in Cody, Wyoming, and decided to go river rafting the next day. But the water was so cold with the spring runoff that everybody froze. That didn't go very well either. So we went to see what other interesting things there were to see. Amazingly the boys (six, eight, and nine) lasted a whole day in the incredible Western Museum they have there and actually enjoyed themselves. I didn't have to pull someone out of a display because he wanted to get a closer look at the weapons, and they didn't get bored and start throwing the Indian spears at each other; it was great.

As I pulled up to the cowboy bar turned restaurant for breakfast, I began to get that sinking feeling that this meal was going to be a disappointing ordeal also. Now, what do I do? Suddenly I got that clear voice inside that I knew was the Lord, *Why don't you pray before you go in.* Hum...pray before we even go inside the restaurant? What do I pray? *Simply pray for good food and good service in Jesus' name. Then believe it will happen as you prayed.* Now that was a huge flashing light kind of revelation for me. I announced to the family that God just showed me what to do about all the bad restaurant experiences we had been having. So I parked and made everybody wait and listen and agree with my simple prayer. The kids all said amen, bounced out of the car, and ran to wait for us at the front door. Do you know what a relief it is to finally get good food and good service after all the bad experiences we had over the last two days? It looked like we got the best waitress in the whole place too! We felt like we were in Breakfast Heaven.

There was not one meal where I didn't pray like that for the rest of the trip. And you know what? It worked every single time. Wow! That was years ago, and we still practice saying that prayer every time we eat out. We even pray for other things, too, when we can tell that we need to. When we pray it, we expect to have a good experience, whatever it may be. Such a simple revelation. Such a simple prayer, but what a profound difference it regularly makes in our lives.

Cliff Diving at La Quebrada, Acapulco

No one believed I could do it; Somehow, I knew not to tell anyone my dream and what I was doing. Actually, I just didn't want to hear any more about what they all thought I couldn't do. So I told no one, not even my best friends, not my brothers or my family. Even my father, who supported me in most things, didn't believe I could do it, so I didn't tell him either. Many friends and family couldn't imagine how such a thing was even possible; some not only didn't believe but were jealous, so jealous they couldn't even be nice about it. Thinking I might do something so big, so grand.

But I had a dream. I was going to dive off of the cliff at Acapulco. It was like a fire in my bones that wouldn't give up until I did it, or at least tried. I'd had this dream since I was about ten. I was born for this; I was created for this. For me, it was my destiny. It wasn't just something I wanted to do; it was something I had to do. It was a dream that I believe the Father had put in my heart, even before I was a Christian. I thought of it often. I never thought of how I would do it or even how I would get there to do it. I mean, it was thousands of miles away in a foreign country. I simply knew I would do it; I never thought I couldn't. The how never mattered. The how was never a problem in my mind. The money, the logistics of how to get there, where to stay, how to prepare, how to know what to do, never entered my mind. So I never dealt with all the "what if you can't do this or that" and "how the heck will you even begin to do any of this anyway?" I simply knew that if I could just get to that cliff that I could dive off of it. And not only that, but that I could do it well. I mean, why not? I'm a diver. It's what I am; it's what I do.

I'd jumped off of some cliffs before, but I'd never been off of anything so big or so treacherous. Something so intimidating that if you miss or do one thing wrong, you can die. If you don't catch the waves just right, you crash into the rocks under the water and die. If you do catch the wave just right, you still have to tuck the dive up quickly, or you will crash into the rocks underwater and die. If you don't control the dive well enough in the air, then when you hit the water, it will break your back, your neck, or your arms. The bottom of the cliff extends twenty-seven feet out, so if you don't jump out far enough to clear the rocks, you will crash and die. If you don't have the experience you need to put all these things together, you will crash and die.

There's something special when you're falling through the air at such a place from such a height. It feels like it's spiritual, like you've entered another dimension of life; it's like you're more alive than you've ever felt or known. I felt a oneness with all of creation. I felt like I would land in the very hands of God. I'd never felt such incredible freedom. Earthly chains were broken. Somehow I'd experienced a touch from heaven. Like He had reached down from heaven and actually touched me. Like

He had shown me a glimpse of His glory. The peace, the power, the joy felt like it was bursting from an unending well within my heart as I hurtled through the air living my dream. Hope fulfilled is powerful.

We, my cousin Harold and my brother Jeff who were both sixteen, and me, I was nineteen, left Denver at the beginning of December in a little Subaru. We were going to be gone for thirty days, and we were driving down the western coast of Mexico, sleeping on the beaches, camping out, spearfishing for food, looking for archeological sites, and anything else interesting that we could explore. Actually, besides the beaches, we ended up sleeping in a number of out-of-the-way hotels and eating a bunch of fantastic meals at little restaurants, and outdoor food stands along the way. The whole trip was an incredible, something new everyday adventure. And no, none of us got sick.

The pineapple/mango juice we got from a street vendor in Guaymas after exploring the old movie set and seaside cliffs to the north was so good; we had to turn around at the end of town and go back and get some more. Okay, a lot more. Señor Pineapple was thrilled as he served them up as fast as we could drink them.

In Guadalajara, I turned the wrong way on a one-way dirt street, and out of nowhere, a big fat Mexican cop with sunglasses and a neatly trimmed handlebar mustache showed up and pulled us over. He walked up to the window, pulled out his 45 and cocked it, and crossed his arms on his stomach, demanding I get out of the car. After a $20 bribe, we were good to go, and he even gladly escorted us to the large outdoor market nearby. He waved goodbye and yelled out the window of his car, joking about one-way streets as we walked towards the colorful fruit and vegetable stands manned by some cute little Indian girls that giggled with delight as we approached them. They had never seen blond, blue-eyed American boys before. They wondered if we could really see out of blue eyes. We had a lot of fun showing them we could. By the time we were ready to leave, they had decided they wanted to marry Harold. You should have seen the look on his face. Priceless!

We met so many interesting characters in Mazatlán that we couldn't remember them all. And the fire-grilled fish and fresh fruit at the beach melted in our mouths.

We had fresh speared red snapper in Puerto Vallarta. I missed the first one and got a blowfish. After a lot of work, we figured out why no one ever ate them. We were using a Hawaiian sling to spear them with.

We spent Christmas Eve in the sleepy little old colonial town of San Blas. The cathedral on the main square was well lit and full of worshipping people singing Spanish Christmas songs. The large old wooden front doors were swung open, and the music floated out into the square bustling with colorfully dressed worshippers. We could feel the peace that came, especially that night of the year, and it was comforting for three boys so far away from home.

Christmas day, we celebrated with a wonderful breakfast at a quaint little place just off the square. The nice family that ran it was enjoyable. Then we explored the old fort on top of the bluff above town, the cannons still resting on the crumbling walls. The road up there was not well used as we followed it through the jungle to the clearing that happened to be the fort. The ancient, well-preserved church of stone was still standing. Though the roof and doors and windows of wood were long gone, and it was beginning to be swallowed up by the jungle. Large green iguanas lay peacefully sunning themselves on the walls near the cannons, songbirds serenaded us from the trees nearby, and the view over the village to the ocean was exceptional.

Then we took a boat deep into the mangrove swamp to a special, clear, cold, freshwater spring. The strange things we saw in the water on the way there made us glad we were safe in a boat. We played for a while there, doing tricks off of a trapeze hanging from a tree into the water and drinking warm Coca-Cola in the pleasant tropical sun. Then we took the boat back through the swamp of mystery to solid, dry ground.

Another cool, misty day as we drove along, Harold found an old Aztec ruin on the map, and we searched until we found it in a farmer's fallow field hidden behind the low-lying clouds. We asked permission from the farmer that lived there and looked around and found all kinds of pottery and implements, especially obsidian knives that had been turned up by the plow. It was a fascinating place. Though we couldn't figure out what the structure really was.

Early evening as we stopped at the next beach to spearfish for our dinner, we were confronted by some concerned local women who grabbed me by my arm to warn us about the "large terrible beasts in the waves that would kill us." "Don't go in this water here; you will never come back out!" They admonished us with great passion. Once we thanked them for their concern, they let go of my arm, satisfied that they had saved us. As we stood there with the women watching the large waves rise and curl over, we could see large, mysterious dark shapes darting through them. The evidence that they were right. Time to go find dinner somewhere else. So we thanked them again, they were very gracious, and we moved on.

Late afternoon on another deserted beach, we found a couple with three cute nieces our age doing the tango to a battery-operated turntable in the sand. What characters they were. What fun we all had. We had stopped to bathe in the ocean and go spearfishing for dinner. But they excitedly convinced us to follow them down to Acapulco to eat with them and spend the night at their house. What gracious hosts they were.

On the way, we were stopped at a checkpoint by the Mexican army. The guy on my side cocked his AK47, stuck it into my ear, and forced us out of the car. It was incredibly tense; each of us had a gun poking us somewhere with an angry-looking Mexican on the other end. We thought for a few moments that we were going to die on a jungle road somewhere north of Acapulco. After we had gotten everything out of the trunk and spread it across the road so they could see if there were any drugs or guns or anything they wanted to take, the uncle walks up, talks to the army guys, and then they smile and motion us on. Whew! Close call. Thank God for helpful, new, influential friends.

Their house had an incredible view from the hill above the bay. The night lights from the houses and ships were like glimmering jewels across the dark sea. Breakfast was American pancakes. The girls giggled at our surprise as they served them to us with some kind of tropical syrup. That was the last thing we expected to eat.

Then down to the local Mexican beach for a playful time filled with swimming, laughter, and yes, more Tango as uncle and auntie twirled and turned, and paused and dipped, for the growing audience, constantly throwing sand in the air as they kicked with their feet.

After saying goodbye to our newfound friends, we spent the next night on a deserted beach south of town, sleeping soundly to the rhythm of the surf crashing a few feet away. The next morning we awoke late; the sun had already risen and was kissing our faces with its warmth. As I lay there with my eyes closed, I knew that it was now or never. If I was ever going to dive off of the cliff at Acapulco, I had to do it this morning. So we gathered our things and headed off looking for the road to the famous cliff as I explained what I intended to do. Harold and Jeff's attitude was, "Okay, let's try and see what happens."

The spectator area is a flat paved area with a metal railing around it. It was still fairly early, so there were no other people there. The cliff rises high above you while the surf surges through the channel between the two sides. It was time to follow through with my plan. I gave the camera to Harold and took my clothes off by the railing. I had my swimsuit underneath. Then I hopped up on the railing and dove the thirty feet or so down into the water. There were three or four incredibly surprised Mexican divers at the water's edge at the bottom of the cliff. When I surfaced near them, the head diver said, "You can't be in here; you aren't allowed to dive off the cliff. Only we are, and we are a small special group that has been trained and knows how to do it."

I said, "Well, you just had the International Competition here, so that means others are allowed to dive here too."

"Yes, but only for competitions. Most people think they can do it, but it is too dangerous. Too many got hurt trying, so we don't allow it anymore."

"Well, I'm a diver, and I know what to do."

"You Americans only do fancy tricks because your shoulders aren't strong enough to just dive in."

"Well, my shoulders are strong enough, and I know I can do it."

"No, you can't."

"Yes, I can."

"No, you can't."

"Yes, I can. As a matter of fact, I've never done this before, but I'll bet you I can do it as good as you can. First time. No practice."

"You could never do it as good as me; I've been diving here for years."

"Yes, I can, and I can even do it better than you."

He was really upset now, as he stood up, waving his arms wildly, and had started spitting while he talked, but his curiosity was piqued, and my challenge to him was more than he could take. "All right, but only if you climb up from here at the bottom rather than walk out at the top," he said, thinking that would deter me.

But I wasn't intimidated, and I wasn't afraid.

"Okay, where do I start?"

"Right there." he pointed to a spot nearby. "And when you get up there, you will find a small place to stand and put your feet.

Remember, if you don't jump out far enough, you'll die on the rocks."

His attitude had lightened up.

None of this was planned; it just happened.

So with that, I swam over to the rock face and began scaling the cliff, barefooted, with them yelling out directions about where to climb from down below. It was not hard for me; it was easy as I had been climbing cliffs since I could remember. I climbed quickly all the way up to the diving spot. It was a tiny carved-out flat spot just big enough to fit your feet in the midst of that massive cliff. I could feel strength literally surging through my body. I was now up at the same height as the birds circling and looking for their next meal, up where the breeze catches their wings, high above the spectators that came out of nowhere and had begun gathering below, high above the churning water.

Turning slowly around so as not to fall down the cliff, I get my first look at the massiveness of the cliff I have to clear, the beauty of the amazing view, and the surf crashing against the rocks far below. Looking down at my feet on the tiny flat spot where I'm standing, I notice blood is dripping from my toes and coloring the stones red underneath me. Hmm...I guess I had cut them on the sharp rocks during the long climb up, but I was so focused I felt no pain, not even now.

The distraction of all the blood allowed fear to pierce my mind; I could even feel it trying to take over my heart. It started shaking me, and thoughts of, *This is stupid, you're going to die!* began to flood through me. So I looked out at the vast ocean to my right and scanned the horizon shrouded in clouds, taking note of the warmth and energy and comfort that I could feel from the tropical sun. In my mind, I simply said no to the fear and began to repeat over and over I can do this; I can do this! I am well able; I can do this! Then I cleared my mind and looked straight out at the birds flying right there with me and began to breathe deeply. Calm came back to me, a peace refilled my mind, and I could again feel the strength surging through my body, my heart pounding in my chest. I surveyed the cliff and the water below and chose a spot to place my dive. I was anxious, but there was no more fear. As I controlled my mind, my focus returned even stronger. I was in such a laser-focused zone that I no longer heard anything but peace, nor did I see anything but what I had come to do. Closing my eyes for a few moments and breathing deeply again, I visualize my dive from start to finish, remembering how much I have to clear before I can even hit the water. Looking at the spot on the water I would aim for, then out at the horizon in front of me, I hold up my arms to balance and help thrust me forward, and I push up and out with all my might.

Thrusting my arms out to the side while stretching my legs backward together and pointing my toes behind me, I hold the dive with perfect control like I've done so many thousands of times before. I'm quickly going so fast the wind is passing ferociously by my ears, and the moisture in my eyes has been pushed out of the corners and is streaming backward towards my head. It feels like an eternity in the air, like time has stopped for me so I can soak in this incredible experience. I pushed out with such force that, at first, it looked like I was going to hit the cliff on the other side. Oh, nuts! I hold my form, hoping I won't.

A few more moments and I realize I'll miss it, but it's going to be close. I can see the spot where I'll hit the water, so now I prepare for the impact of the entry.

Moving my arms forward to prepare for entry, I make fists to pound it open and move my head, so I catch it at the perfect angle at the top of my forehead. That way, it doesn't snap your neck as you break the surface.

Tucking it up and flipping around immediately after I'm underwater so I don't slam into the rocky bottom, I pause about seven feet under the water. After those intense moments with the loud air screaming through my ears as I hurtled towards the water, there is silence, and the silence is incredible though almost eerie, I'm suddenly in another world. I relax every muscle in my body momentarily and just float underwater, listening to the shells and small rocks clicking and clanking against the bottom as the surf surges back and forth. It helps release the build-up from the incredible intensity of the dive just moments before.

Shooting to the surface for a deep breath of air, I thrust my fist in the air for victory, sweet victory. More tourists than before who seemingly came out of nowhere are leaning over the rail, cheering, clapping, and whistling their approval. I felt like a real rock star, and I wasn't even doing it for them. Heck, I was so focused I didn't even see them until now. The Mexican divers over on the rocks at the bottom of the cliff are smiling; I had won their respect and approval. I didn't expect that from them, but I sure welcomed it now. Before I can bask completely in this accomplishment, I decide to do it again. One more time, because this is the only opportunity I'll ever have, and I'm making the most of it. So I scale the cliff and do it again. How sweet hope fulfilled is. How exhilarating it is to accomplish a lifelong dream. I have witnesses, and Harold took the pictures to prove it.

We celebrated by eating a nice breakfast at an open-air restaurant with the sound of seagulls crying out and a view of the vast ocean below. We had taken our time and enjoyed the trip getting down there so much that we only had a few days left to make it back in time for school. So we hopped in the car and headed home.

Dream accomplished. Dream fulfilled.

But now that this dream has been accomplished, I need a new dream, maybe even two or three.

I just want to encourage anyone reading this that no matter what your dream is, go for it! There will always be more who don't believe you can do it than do believe that you can. There will always be more excuses why it will never work or never happen than reasons why you can do it. But for you, it starts in your heart. Begin now to take some steps in that direction, even if it's only in your mind, and keep the dream to yourself and if you must tell someone, only tell those you can trust with your heart. You don't need to hear from the naysayers why you can't; you need to be encouraged that you can.

So whoever you are,

I believe in you.

Whatever your dream,

I believe you can do it.

And with the added blessing that comes with being a Christian,

with the wisdom that only the Holy Spirit can give you,

I believe you can do it,

even if you fall a few times trying,

just try, just try, just try,

you can do it.

And the Father God who gave you the dream

will help you to fulfill it.

Make the decision that you will do it,

that you will begin.

Make that decision.

Now.

Which Door, Which Path?

One door swinging open.
One door slamming closed.
I'm looking for the answer.
The one I need to know.

It all should be so clear now,
but it's shrouded in a fog.
I see lights shining through it;
I know it won't be long.

Open up my eyes to see.
My ears to hear the truth.
My mind to understand it all.
Give me wisdom, wisdom too.

Like the sunlight in the morning.
It's all becoming clear.
As understanding rises.
There's nothing now to fear.

The path opens before me.
The Lord also draws near.
What once was tangled jungle
is now direction true and clear.

Open up my eyes to see.
My ears to hear the truth.
My mind to understand it all.
Give me wisdom, wisdom too.

The Proposal

I had just dropped Michelle off and was basking in the afterglow of an especially enjoyable evening. Suddenly this voice speaks out loud from behind me and slightly to the right side, "If you pass this one up, you'll regret it the rest of your life."

"What!" I exclaim, shocked at what I'd just heard. I slammed on the brake and stopped in the middle of the cold winter road and turned around to see who was speaking. But no one was there. *Hmm...that's weird*, I said to myself, and I started driving down the road again.

Then I heard the voice speak out again, "If you pass this one up, you'll regret it the rest of your life." I jerked my head around again to see who was speaking; no one there. Then I realized that with the statements came this sudden instant knowledge He was talking about Michelle. I also somehow knew it was the Lord talking out loud to me. A great peace and comfort settled upon me. Nothing like this had ever happened to me before, and since then, I've only heard God's audible voice a few times. Most of the time, I have found that along with Scripture, He leads me by peace, or an inner prompting, or an impression, or that still small voice down in my heart.

In my mind, I was a long way from thinking anything about marriage. I hadn't even considered it. Our relationship had become a wonderful friendship, and it was getting better all the time. Michelle was fun and always enjoyable to be around, and we were becoming best friends; we were spending a lot more time with each other and had started doing many things together. We would laugh and talk for hours and never get tired of each other and then look forward to the next time we could be together. But *marriage*? The ten-minute drive to my house seemed like it took a lifetime as I pondered what had just happened, what had been said. Then I realized that I had started to fall in love with her. No, actually, I was in love with her. How did I not know this already? Wow, I'm going to have to think about this for a while; I need to process what just happened. I need to process these feelings in my heart.

By the time I pulled up into my driveway after that seemingly long drive home, I had decided, well, I'm going to do it, I would ask Michelle to marry me. I loved her; I realized that now, and I didn't want to miss out on the best and most wonderful person and opportunity of my life. What a great wife she would make. What a great friend and lover she would be. I realized now that I wanted to spend the rest of my life with her. I was excited. But I had no clue when, or how, or what it looked like. Plus, I was going to need some confirmation of some sort, something to let me know without a shadow of a doubt that this was right. That she felt the same way about us as I did. I mean, if she didn't feel the same way about us, then it didn't matter at all. So I went about the next few weeks waiting for the right timing and not thinking about it too much. I just knew that I would know it when I saw it, whenever that was.

I had asked Michelle to come to meet some friends of mine that lived up Golden Gate Canyon. Long ago, he had purchased the land and built the home of his dreams for him and his wife. Their name was Vigil. He was a wise old Basque sheepherder that had come to America with the hope of a better life and to follow his dreams. He and his brother bought some cheap land with good grass and water up in Wyoming and were minding their own business tending a growing sheep herd and starting their American dream. When out of nowhere, an energy company offered them millions of dollars for their simple ranch because just beneath the surface was a huge deposit of high-quality coal. Hmm...keep herding sheep or become an instant millionaire? What a choice! Being the good businessmen that they were, they took the money, came to Colorado, invested wisely, and were living well, and had been for many years.

Long ago, an unusually large snowstorm stranded many people in Golden. My grandparents had a hotel with two restaurants on main street. All the rooms were full, yet the cold, stranded, weary people kept coming in looking for something warm to drink, food, and hopefully a place to stay, but there was no more room at the Inn. The staff was stuck too. The roads were impassable. No one could make it home. If they weren't parked already, the people were leaving their cars where they had become stuck on the roads and were trudging through the snow to our place.

Rather than turn anyone away, my grandfather had told our people to give them whatever they wanted to drink on the house and only charge them for the food they ordered. He made sure everything kept running like a clock as huge quantities of food and drink flowed out of the kitchen, and the dirty dishes came back in. Soon all the seats in the lobby, the coffee shop, the lounge, and the dining room were filled, and there was standing room only. So he opened the five banquet rooms so that people might have a place to sit, and soon even they were all filled too. Even the floor of the hallway to the back rooms was full of people sitting down, shaking off the cold. My grandparents still chose not to turn anyone away; they just made room. It was getting late now, and the weary people were starting to lay down on the floor, trying to cover themselves with their coats. Some used their shoes for pillows. So, my grandmother had the staff break out all the spare bedding and handed it out to the people, one blanket per couple to keep warm and then sheets when the blankets ran out until there were no more left. She walked around with the staff handing out blankets, pouring hot coffee, and laughing, joking, and encouraging everyone. Her laugh was one of those truly infectious, feel-good, happy laughs that you could always hear from the other rooms. When I was little, all I had to do to tell where she was, was to listen for her laugh. Like it says in proverbs, "A merry heart does good like medicine." Her encouragement worked like medicine, and pretty soon, she had the whole place calmed down, and the folks were looking forward to enduring this temporary hardship with a good attitude and then moving on once the storm broke.

Vigil and his wife were among those who were stuck here in this predicament and, like most everyone else, truly appreciated the hospitality and left, never forgetting how well they had all been treated. My grandparents single-handedly inspired a small army of people to go out and bless others when hardship falls upon them.

Vigil never forgot, and when he found out who I was, he went out of his way to bless me and include me in special events he created with the important and famous people he knew. How interesting, my grandparent's act of blessing people was returned not to them but to me. I got to benefit from their kindness to others. That's a lesson I treasure, and I will never forget.

Anyway, over the years, I developed a nice relationship with this interesting and wonderful couple that were old enough to be my grandparents.

As I called out to them from their gate, no one answered; they couldn't hear me inside their mountain mansion, but their Great Dane sure did. They had bought them as trained guard dogs, and they came aggressively barking to the large wrought iron gate, sticking their muzzles through the bars to get a better sniff of who we were. I sized them up carefully and saw that we could walk through them if, and only if, we showed no fear.

So I told Michelle what we were going to do. She responded that there was no way she could do that; she didn't want to be eaten. And besides, how do you not show fear, especially when you know you're afraid? Not taking no for an answer, I explained that as we walked, she wasn't to look them in the face, especially in the eyes, and just look forward no matter how close or intimidating they got. To stay right with me and not trail even one step behind. "You might be afraid; just don't show it." I knew we would make it; I could see into the dogs and tell that we could.

If, and only if, she stayed right with me and followed my lead. I had faith in her; I knew that she could do it.

I unlatch the gate and turn and tell her, "Okay, let's go, don't think about it, just walk with me and stay right with me, and we'll be all right." Opening the gate and stepping in confidently and shutting it behind us, I say, "Follow me," and we take off. The dog's big wet noses were about the same height as our heads, so when they barked, it was right into our ears. Their hot breath pummeled our faces every time they barked, with small amounts of dog spit splattering on our necks and the sides of our heads. Sometimes I could feel a wet nose slide across my ear. "Don't look! Don't look at them! Don't show fear! They can smell the fear, and they will attack if they do, so don't, or we're both in trouble."

"Oh God," Michelle cried out as she buried her face between my shoulders; it was almost more than she could bear. But she did it, and she did it trying her best not to show fear. She simply kept her face in my back, her eyes down at the ground, and only moved her feet with mine. My confidence and boldness carried us both to the front door. But I was only that confident because I had seen that it could be done; otherwise, there would have been no way I would have tried it. By the time we got there, about a thirty-yard walk through the barking and sometimes snarling guard dogs, Michelle was doing better because she realized we were doing it, and it also seemed as though the dogs started to wonder by then if we weren't friends. Once she saw we were actually going to make it, the fear started to lift up off of her.

You should have seen the look on Vigil's face when he opened the door and saw it was me and that we had just walked through his vicious dogs without being harmed. He was thrilled to see me and shocked that we had made it to the front door without being eaten. I was shone later in a dream that the Lord had been with us, protecting us the whole way and that He was the one who had given me the ability to read the dogs correctly. To know if they would attack or not. To know if we would be safe.

Taking us on a tour of his home that was created like a castle, he took great joy in Michelle's reactions to the treasures and beauty inside. In the great room adorned with ancient European tapestries and other art, he paused and said, "Watch this." He pushed a button, and the elegant curtains at the end of the room parted, revealing a fifteen-foot tall, forty-foot-wide wall of specially partitioned glass looking out to the mountainside with its bubbling creek below. "Do you know what this wall of glass really is?" he asked. She didn't. So I explained, while he stood by proudly beaming with joy, that it's a huge exact replica of the background of a painting of Jesus hanging on the cross by Salvador Dalí. I was the only person in the whole thirty years he had it that knew what the window was. (I had studied art in Italy, that's why.) Every time he looks at that beautiful view through his special window, he says he is reminded of what Jesus did for us all. Wow, pretty interesting, huh?

As we talked about art and history, he guided us to a very comfortable nook by a window where we all could sit together. With typical gracious European hospitality, his wife brought a special bottle of wine for us to share in some incredibly beautiful royal blue wine glasses. They were so beautiful; they were stunning. He explained in eloquent detail how he had them created just for him. He wouldn't allow anyone else to drink until I had sampled his special wine in the special glasses and approved. Then he raised his glass and made a toast that was actually a blessing over us.

As we sat enjoying our unique surroundings, good conversation, and the fellowship of friends, we noticed the snow had begun falling softly out the window. Mr. Vigil sat up, and with the sincerity of a father to his son, said, "Mr. Greg" (he always called me Mr. Greg). Then extending his hand out towards Michelle, he said, "This one is a keeper; you should marry this one." Shocked and not sure what to do or say, I instantly knew that this was the other confirmation I needed about what the Lord had said in my car, telling me not to pass this one up, or I would regret it the rest of my life. You just never know how the Lord is going to confirm things for you.

Looking over at Michelle, her eyes gleaming with light, she nodded her head in approval towards me; she was agreeing; she was silently saying yes. Knowing now that this was it, she really was the one, and that now was the time, I heard myself say, "Yes, Mr. Vigil, you are right; she is a keeper."

Looking out the window for a moment at the snow that was falling more strongly now, Mr. Vigil turns to me and says in his Basque accent, "Mr. Greg, let us finish our wine so you may leave before the storm makes it hard for you to return home."

After saying our thank yous and goodbyes and seeing that the guard dogs were no longer a threat, Michelle and I playfully tossed snow at each other and got into the car. Ours would be the only tracks on the road. As I was getting in the car, I could feel this incredible compulsion to do it now, to ask her now. There was also this peace like I had in the car the night the Lord spoke to me, along with a comfortable feeling of warmth that seemed to hug me. I struggled with myself for what seemed eons of time, but I knew it was only a few seconds to build up the courage, and then I just did it. I looked over at her and asked, "Will you marry me? Will you be my wife?".

To my great surprise, she responded with a joyful, "I thought you would never ask. Yes!" In that car, in the softly falling snow, and the incredible peace and silence that come only with a gentle winter storm, I kissed her, then we drove off, off into the future.

It was almost an hour's drive back to her place, and by then, we had everything figured out. We were leaving in eighteen days for a two-week vacation in Tahiti. Why don't we get married before we leave, and then Tahiti can be our honeymoon? So Michelle took care of her dress and the cake, the flowers, and the music, and I took care of the rest. We had the wedding in two weeks, invited 300 people, and you know what? Everybody showed up. I mean everybody! My cowboy uncle, who had a small cowboy congregation, even drove all the way up from New Mexico to marry us. The whole thing came off without a hitch, well, other than Uncle Lewis forgetting Michelle's name, and then the music girl that couldn't sing. Thankfully no one could hear her bad voice or the music anyway because the sound system wasn't working right. And on a Tuesday evening of all things, amazing, huh? And on Saint Paddy's Day at that!

When I found the perfect place to get married, at a church with a majestic and breathtakingly beautiful view of the continental divide behind the pulpit, the best day of the week for them was a Tuesday which also just happened to be Saint Patrick's Day. What an incredible, God-ordained coincidence. For an Irish boy, I can't think of a better day. The Holy Spirit has a great sense of humor, and He layered it with prophetic promises just for us.

And guess what our favorite gift was? That very set of specially made royal blue wine glasses. The Vigils gave us their whole set! What a heart! What a wonderful gift with a deep, special meaning just for us.

Anyway, I wonder how long it would have taken for me to realize I was in love and ask Michelle to marry me if the Lord hadn't spoken to me when He did. For Him to have to speak to me out loud like He did shows me I was probably headed in the wrong direction and didn't even know it. I was amazed that God cared for us enough to speak to me in a way that got my attention and helped me make the right decision about Michelle and me. I'm so glad He did; life has been a wonderful adventure with Michelle, my best friend and the love of my life ever since. Yes, the love of my life ever since.

"Thanks, Lord, for getting us started on the right foot."

So with that, let me offer an Irish blessing
to all who are reading this:

"May all your decisions be based on the truth.
May the love in your heart not be hidden
and,
As you slide down the banister of life,
May all the splinters be turned in the other direction."

A Wilderness Prayer

Oh Lord my God,
I lift up my heart to You.
I lift up my heart to You.
I have sown my seed in the morning
and in the evening alike.
I do not know which one will succeed
or whether both of them alike will be good.
Oh, Father, I have done everything,
I have done all that the situation demands
and I stand,
I stand firm
believing your promises,
believing your word,
that you change the wilderness of my life
into a pool of water
and the dry land of my hope into springs of water.
Thank You that You hear me
for I know that I shall stand
and I shall see the salvation of the Lord
because You are with me in this trouble
and I know that You will rescue me;
may You rescue me today.
Fill my mind with Your light,
the light of Your truth that
gives me hope
and sets me free.

From Psalm 107:35, Ephesians 6:13, Psalm 91:15, Ecclesiastes
11:6, 1 Samuel 12:16, Psalm 119:130, and James 1:5.

About the Author

Greg Holland was trained from the time he was young as a cowboy/chef/entrepreneur growing up on a cattle ranch and running his grandparent's hotel and restaurant in town called the Holland House. He studied art in Europe, was an exchange student in Mexico, and loves history. His eclectic background makes it easier for him to relate to many different people and cultures.

He has heard God's voice most of his life and has spent years speaking destiny, hope, and healing into people's lives. Greg and Michelle have been married since 1981 and have three children and one grandchild.

CPSIA information can be obtained
at www.ICGtesting.com
Printed in the USA
LVHW020713160222
711266LV00008B/409